Aubrey L. Moore

Holy Week Addresses

delivered at S. Paul's Cathedral in Holy Week, 1888

Aubrey L. Moore

Holy Week Addresses
delivered at S. Paul's Cathedral in Holy Week, 1888

ISBN/EAN: 9783337285760

Printed in Europe, USA, Canada, Australia, Japan

Cover: Foto ©Lupo / pixelio.de

More available books at **www.hansebooks.com**

HOLY WEEK ADDRESSES

Holy Week Addresses

on

I. The Appeal and the Claim of Christ
II. The Words from the Cross

DELIVERED AT

S. PAUL'S CATHEDRAL

IN HOLY WEEK, 1888

BY

AUBREY L. MOORE, M.A.

Honorary Canon of Christ Church, Oxford
Examining Chaplain to the Lord Bishop of Oxford
Tutor of Keble and Magdalen Colleges

NEW EDITION

LONDON
LONGMANS, GREEN, & CO.
AND NEW YORK: 15 EAST 16th STREET
1893

PREFACE

THE first four of the addresses in the present volume were given in the earlier days of Holy Week, to an audience composed mainly of men, and were intended to be of a less popular, and at least implicitly of a more argumentative character, than those given on Good Friday. It seemed impossible to publish them without a few words of explanation, especially in reference to the last of the four addresses.

The underlying assumption is that faith is the act of the whole man, and therefore that, if the revelation of God in Christ is a true object of faith, it must appeal to and claim the affections, the will, and the reason.

Such a view, obvious as it may seem to some, is diametrically opposed to the theology which has long been popular, and which is only gradually losing its hold on the minds of Englishmen. Since the Reformation, scientific, as opposed to biblical, theology in England has been mainly Calvinistic. In an interesting article, contributed just a quarter of a century ago to the *Christian Remembrancer*, the writer, speaking of the various religious systems in England, says, "Their differences are quite subordinate. All are agreed in the main. There is, in truth, but one theological system accepted by all; we mean Calvinistic Protestantism. Even within the Church, where there is the counteracting influence of Catholic ideas from the Prayerbook, Calvinism may almost be said to predominate. Not only is it the only theology of the Low Church party, but many of its ideas are more or less accepted by High Churchmen. In fact, with the exception of those who have been thoroughly influenced by the Catholic movement, every intelligent Englishman will instinctively look at Christianity from the Calvinistic point of view."[1]

Whether this fairly represents the state of theology at the time or not, it certainly is

[1] *Christian Remembrancer*, January, 1863, p. 27.

quite untrue in the present day. Not only has the number of "those who have been thoroughly influenced by the Catholic movement" largely increased, but Calvinism has come to be discredited all round, and is giving way either to a truer view of Christian theology, or to one of the numerous forms of belief which range from the old Socinianism to a theism hardly distinguishable from pantheism. It is probable that nobody now accepts iterally the Westminster Confession. The nonconforming sects are rapidly abandoning all that is distinctive of Calvinism.[1] The protest as yet is mainly a protest of the heart and conscience. No view which represents the love of God as selective, not universal, can in our day secure a hearing. One of the noblest protests against the immorality of the Calvinistic theory of the Atonement comes from a representative Nonconformist, Dr. Dale. The doctrine of predestination to damnation, whether as formulated in the "Institutes" (bk. iii. ch. xxiii.)

---

[1] See Dr. Clifford's article on "Baptist Theology," *Contemporary Review*, April, 1888; and his address from the chair of the Baptist Union.

a plea for a Christian rationalism—that is to say, for a scientific treatment of what is revealed; a Christian philosophy which, starting from within the atmosphere of faith, will bring the eternal facts of revealed truth into relation, not only with one another, but with our present ways of thinking, and our present knowledge of nature and of man. There is a rationalism which is unchristian and a rationalism which is a Christian duty, just as there is a scepticism which paralyzes reason and a scepticism which is a condition of scientific progress. Catholic Christianity represents God as knowable, and reverently yet fearlessly, not as an interesting speculation, but as a religious duty, attempts to interpret and give a reason for His acts in the light of His revelation of Himself. Calvinism, in its over-anxiety to defend the majesty of God, makes Him unknowable by representing His actions in religion as defiantly unlike what conscience would have them be, and no less defiantly unlike what reason finds His acts to be in the world of visible nature. There is surely no greater obstacle to the faith of a real student of nature than the discovery that

PREFACE. xi

the God of popular Christianity is the antithesis of order, of law, of intelligibility.[1]

No attempt is made in these addresses to answer the question how far Calvin is himself responsible for modern and popular Calvinism, or how far the Westminster Confession is binding on modern Calvinists. The main lines of Calvinism are not easily obscured, even by well-meaning explanations. The Lambeth Articles of 1593, the attempt at the Hampton Court Conference to add these as 'the nine assertions orthodoxical"[2] to the English Articles, the futile attempt by the Westminster Assembly to revise the Thirty-nine Articles in a Calvinistic sense,[3] and the subsequent abandonment of them in favour of the Westminster Confession, show clearly what Calvinism in England and Scotland is in contrast to the authorized teaching of the Anglican Church. That much which was once considered essential in Calvinism is now openly discarded by professing Calvinists, is

---

[1] Professor H. Drummond's "Natural Law" owes its fascination mainly, perhaps, to its attempt to make a theology which will fit into the categories of physical science.

[2] Lawrence's Bampton Lectures, p. 8, note.

See Neale, " History of Puritans," vol. iii. App. vii.

a matter of which Churchmen at all events have little ground to complain.

Against the statement that "Calvinism begat Agnosticism" (p. 37), exception may, of course, be taken. It may be urged, as it has recently been urged by Dr. Martineau, that "for much of the Agnosticism of the age the Gnosticism of theologians is undeniably responsible."[1] But, so far from disputing this statement, it seems to me to be obviously true. Yet it is equally true, though less obvious, that for much of the Gnosticism of the age the Agnosticism of theologians is undeniably responsible. For the two react upon each other, and intensify each other by reaction. Calvinism and Agnosticism represent respectively the devout and the despairing expression of the belief that God is unknowable to natural reason. Yet it is undoubtedly true that the early and more devout Agnosticism was a protest against, and a reaction from, a mediæval Gnosticism. For, in the later scholastic age, Christian theology had parted itself into two streams, the one Gnostic, the other implicitly Agnostic,

[1] "Study of Religion," vol. i., preface, p. xi.

though both flowed within the territory of the Catholic Church. The *crede ut intelligas* of earlier days became either *intellige ut credas* on the one hand, or *credo quia non rationale* on the other. It would not be difficult to show how Calvinism logically affiliates itself to the latter mode of thinking; and, from fear of rationalism, discountenances and discourages any attempt to explain to reason the great facts of the Christian revelation. They are to be accepted, not inquired into. Even morality tends to become "positive," not "natural." A thing is right or wrong because God enjoins or forbids it. In technical language, *voluntas* is exalted above *intellectus*. On such a view, the "moral difficulties of the Old Testament" rapidly disappear. It becomes quite easy to "justify Jael." Only in the process we have destroyed morality. Similarly, predestination to damnation, which Calvin himself admits to be a "dreadful decree,"[1] must be accepted, however it may shock our moral nature, and

[1] "Decretum quidem horribile fateor; inficiari tamen nemo poterit quia præsciverit Deus quem exitum esset habiturus homo, antequam ipsum conderet, et ideo præsciverit, quia decreto suo sic ordinaverat" ("Instit.," lib. iii. cap. 23, § 7).

our sense of justice. For the clay may not criticize the potter. God's decrees are absolute, and if they are His they are right. Such a view raises the protest of the intellectual as well as the moral nature. " Talis electio sine causis videtur tyrannica," wrote Melancthon.[1] The moral nature revolts against the " tyranny," the reason against the irrationality of such a selection. In practice, indeed, different persons may find the doctrine " full of unspeakable comfort," or may be led to " wretchlessness of most unclean living ; " but God's choice, being in either case unconditioned, is irrational and unmeaning, and reason is driven back to nature, which at least is rational and full of meaning, and does not resent, but rewards the desire to know. And so Calvinism paves the way for Agnosticism. For a theology which affronts and insults that reason, which, after all, is God's gift and not the devil's, drives men to a science which knows not God ; and believers who piously

---

[1] Melancthon, Opera, vol. iii. p. 683, with which Archbishop Lawrence (Bampton Lectures, p. 365) compares the following passage from Bullinger's *Comm. in Rom.*, p. 61 : "Velle enim Dei non est tyrannica quædam et herilis licentia, de qua poeta, ' Sic volo, sic jubeo, sit pro ratione voluntas ; ' sed Dei voluntas justissima et æquissima est."

represent God as irrational, cannot refuse to share the blame with unbelievers who defiantly declare that He is unknowable.

The great need of the day would seem to be, not a new theology, but a Christian philosophy,[1] to do for us in our own language what scholasticism did for the Middle Age, and bring the unchanging Faith, once for all delivered to the saints, into rational connection with our modern knowledge, and our modern ways of thinking. But such a constructive work presupposes the abandonment of the common view that God's truth, because it is His truth, is no proper object for reverent and rational investigation. There is much, surely, which Christianity has yet to claim and absorb and assimilate, not only in the discoveries of the modern science of nature, but in those great systems of Oriental thought, of which we now know so much. But to claim and assimilate implies two things, and they are both of them rare— knowledge and courage ; knowledge of what

[1] It is interesting to find the chairman of the Baptist Union, in his address, recognizing this fact. "In my judgment," he says, "if I may be allowed to say it, one of our needs at this hour is a God-inspired theologian—an Athanasius or Augustine, a Calvin or Arminius" (p. 41).

Christ's revelation is, as a making known to man of the real nature of God; courage to believe that the Faith can afford to face the rational problem, because it holds the Truth. It is no wonder that reasoning men refuse to accept a truth which they must not try to understand; it is no wonder that the unnatural separation of faith from reason has for its result the atrophy of the one, the paralysis of the other.

Of the Good Friday Addresses, there is nothing special to say. They are largely indebted to the various series of similar addresses which have recently been published. They are now printed in the form in which they were delivered at S. Paul's, but, in substance, the addresses are the same as when given at All Saints', Margaret Street, in 1885, and at S. Martin's, Scarborough, last year. They will have more than done their work if, by God's grace, they remind any of those who may have heard them delivered, of some truth learned before the Cross, or some resolution made in the power of the Crucified.

A. L. M.

OXFORD,
Whitsuntide, 1888.

CONTENTS

I.
	PAGE
THE APPEAL AND THE CLAIM OF CHRIST	1

II.
THE APPEAL TO THE AFFECTIONS AND THE HEART   10

III.
THE APPEAL TO THE CONSCIENCE AND THE WILL   21

IV.
THE APPEAL TO THE REASON 30

The Words from the Cross.

INTRODUCTION	45
I. THE PRIEST IN INTERCESSION	50
II. THE PRIEST IN ABSOLUTION	57
III. THE PRIEST IN BLESSING	63
IV. THE SEPARATION	69
V. THE LONGING	75
VI. THE TRIUMPH	81
VII. REST IN GOD	87

The Appeal and the Claim of Christ.

I.

The Appeal and the Claim of Christ.

WE have come apart in this Holy Week, away from our business or our pleasure, to be alone a little while with God before the Cross of Christ. What have we come to see? What do we hope to learn? What is the appeal to which, by our being here, we profess ourselves ready to listen? It is the appeal of God to the creatures He has made, the appeal of the Son of Man to His brethren, the appeal of Divine love to our love. And it is an appeal to our whole nature as well as to all mankind. "I, if I be lifted up from the earth, will draw all men unto Myself."[1]

It comes to us first, that appeal of the Cross, as the appeal of *love*. "Saw ye ever sorrow like unto My sorrow?" "Greater love hath no man than this, that a man lay down his life for his friends." It is an appeal to

[1] S. John xii. 32.

our feelings, our emotions, our affections,—to all that in Bible language is called the heart. But it is more than this. Excited feelings, roused sympathy, admiration of a noble or heroic act, may be transient as a morning cloud, if there is no appeal to the conscience and the will; if it do not make us go forth stronger to live our life in the spirit of the Crucified, to battle for the right, to kill down what is evil and corrupt around us and within. And, then—since man is not only a creature that feels and acts, but is, just because he is man, a reasoning being, and cannot but ask Why?—the appeal must go further yet. It must justify itself to the reason, no less than to the heart and will. It is "reasonable service" that God would have from those whom He has made reasoning beings.

But the appeal of Christ is more than an appeal; it is a *claim*. It is this which constitutes the uniqueness of the appeal. "Ye are not your own; ye are bought with a price." And as the appeal is an appeal to the whole man, so the claim is a claim to the surrender of the whole man—his affections, his will, his reason—to One Who is Perfect Man as well as Very God.

How is that possible? Are there not

hundreds and hundreds, who, even if they feel the appeal, resent the claim; who can recognize, indeed, the heroism of a martyr's death, and sympathize with the undeserved suffering of Him Who went about doing good, but yet cannot recognize in Christ Him Who has taken human nature unto God, and therefore, in the doctrine of the Atonement, see nothing but a theory which shocks alike their conscience and their reason? Look a little deeper, and you will see that the God Whose claim they resent, Whose appeal they will not listen to, is not our God, not the God of the Bible and the Church, but a God fashioned by man to save a theory. For more than two centuries, a dark cloud has rested upon Christian theology in England, and the great central truth, that God is Love, so long obscured, is coming back to men as almost a new discovery. And, meanwhile, souls have been repelled from the life of Faith,—driven often, by the very nobleness of their moral nature or the earnestness of their love of truth, to abandon that false Christianity, and work out, as they think, their own salvation away from the Cross.

The God of popular Calvinism, the God whom arrogant unbelief so often ridicules, is not the God of the Christian Church, but a God unloving, unjust, irrational, who is the antithesis to what is best, most noble, most Divine, in man, and who therefore cannot claim man's allegiance and his love.

In the three addresses which will intervene between to-day and Good Friday, my object will be to try and show what God is, as revealed in Christ; that His claim is the claim of One Who is Perfect Love, and Whose love, as revealed to us from Calvary, is both righteous and ordered by eternal law; that His claim upon our heart, our conscience, and our reason, is the claim of One Who is the *Object of Love*, the *Ideal of Goodness*, the *Perfect Truth*. Because He is this, He appeals to and claims the fidelity of our whole nature, most true to itself when most true to Him, the submission of our reason, the allegiance of our will, the surrender of love. From first to last it is the appeal of love, as the Cross from first to last is the revelation of love. But it is the love of God which contains in itself what human love so often lacks—both justice and reasonableness. For these are structural principles in Perfect Love, and the love which has them not, is not really love.

But behind the appeal of the Cross there is

that which makes it a claim. It is because Christ has been offered up as a Sacrifice *for* us, that He establishes His claim to self-sacrifice *from* us. And if we are to appreciate and respond to the appeal, and recognize the claim of Christ over our lives, we must realize what He has done for us, why the claim of Christ from the Cross is a unique claim, greater even than the claim of the Creator over the creatures He has made.

That is why, year by year, as Lent comes round, we are brought face to face with the mystery of sin—that mystery without which the sacrifice on Calvary were more than mysterious,—impossible and unintelligible. Christianity takes for granted the full-grown desire for God, the full-grown consciousness of sin. It is this contradiction which it solves,— this dualism in our nature which it claims to have removed. The God our heart longs for is the Judge our conscience fears. And yet the Christian, with his eye resting on the Cross of Calvary, is bold to say, "There is therefore now no condemnation to them which are in Christ Jesus." The Incarnation of the Son of God, and the Atonement wrought by Him, are meaningless, unreasonable things to those who know nothing of that spiritual need which Christ came to satisfy. No fact, however true, is intelligible apart from its conditions. It must be unmeaning and unreal. And if we have never felt the longing to give ourselves to God, and the pain of alienation from Him, it cannot be that we shall understand the claim that is based on what Christ has done.

See what the problem of religion is. Man feels and knows that he belongs to God; that his home is heaven, not earth; that his life is the life of the Spirit, not of the flesh; that his true companions are saints and angels, rather than the beasts of the field. In the language of the Bible and of Christian theology, he knows that he was "made in the image of God." But no less surely does he feel and know, antecedently to and apart from all that we call revelation, that there is a barrier which separates him from his God— a barrier which he did not raise, and for which, nevertheless, he feels mysteriously responsible. He recognizes it in the struggle which goes on within him, in the weakness of his will, the darkness of his understanding, the weary, desultory warfare with pride and selfishness and defiling sin, the disorder of his whole being. And all down the history of man, we find the craving for some sacrifice among the deepest instincts of the religious life of the race. Man dare not offer himself, for he knows himself defiled; and so he looks around for that which is purer than himself, and offers it, if perchance it may be acceptable to God. Nothing is too precious or too pure for such a purpose; the firstlings of the flock, the lamb without spot or blemish, nay, the innocent and well-beloved child, must be bound on the altar of sacrifice. What did it all mean? It was a true teaching of experience that man could not save himself, could not think or will himself into the life of God, could not "drift into it on the tide of time." It was a true instinct which sought for reconciliation through sacrifice, for salvation from outside man. In the light which streams from Calvary we see the problem and its solution. "The blood of bulls and goats" could not take away sins. They were empty unreal, barren, those older sacrifices; but not meaningless, for they were "shadows of the true," pointing forward to the One Offering, the Eternal Priest, the Divine Victim.

And all down the Christian ages, one fact stands out conspicuous, one truth enshrined for ever in the Christian consciousness, that by the Death of Christ there has been offered, once and for all, "a full, perfect, and sufficient sacrifice" for the sins of the whole world. Again and again has the fact been overlaid, obscured, travestied by so-called "theories" of the Atonement; but the fact itself stands out as the central thought in the writing of Evangelist and Apostle, the central point in the worship of the Church, the central truth in the practical theology of every Christian soul. "Who is he that condemneth? It is Christ that died." "There is therefore now no condemnation to them which are in Christ Jesus."

Has, then, the Sacrifice of Christ upon the Cross for us made the offering of ourselves unnecessary? God forbid. Rather it has made it *possible*, for it has made it *valid:* and if possible, then natural,—the almost instinctive answer of redeemed humanity. "He died for all," says S. Paul, "that they which live should not henceforth live unto themselves, but unto Him which died for them." The offering up of man to God, so impossible while the burden of sin rested on the conscience, becomes now a holy offering in Christ. Christianity from the first has been deceiving and deceived, if the Death of

Christ was not the setting loose of powers of self-sacrifice which all through the pre-Christian ages were struggling to be free. If man is free now to offer up himself to God, it is because in Christ humanity is gathered up, its past atoned for, its present consecrated, its future claimed.

"Christ our Passover is sacrificed for us," that in Him we may offer up ourselves. As *Love*, as *Goodness*, and as *Truth*, He claims our heart, our will, our reason, that our whole nature, self-surrendered to Him, may be offered up, as once in promise and in type He offered it upon the Cross, a sacrifice well-pleasing unto God, the offering of love to Perfect Love.

II.

The Appeal to the Affections and the Heart.

THE appeal of Christ from the Cross comes to us from the first as a distinctly *human* appeal. It is because we are moral beings that we can recognize the moral beauty of Christ's Death,—its heroic devotion, its self-sacrificing love. Even if in that Death and Passion we ourselves were not concerned, we should be less than men if we did not turn aside to see that great sight—the Death of One Who died for others, Who gave Himself for those He loved. We cannot, even the least emotional among us, gaze unmoved upon such a scene. It is so unlike what we see around us in nature and in man, and yet appeals so naturally to what is best and noblest and most human in us.

(1) What is it which constitutes the strength of that appeal? First, surely, the fact that the suffering was *voluntarily undertaken for the*

sake of others. Nature shrinks from suffering, and would gladly escape from pain. There is suffering enough, God knows, in this world of ours, and all the machinery of our civilization, all the powers of our art and science, are directed to the removal or mitigation of it. There is suffering enough in nature. All down the scale of animated being we can note suffering, and vicarious suffering too. The many suffer and die, that the few may live and prosper. But they do not suffer willingly, or with that end in view. They fight and strive, each for himself. They yield only when they are vanquished by the stronger. There is, so far as we can see, no pity, no remorse, no care for others, no unwillingness to use to the uttermost every advantage they can win. And if ever in the animal world outside man we see an act of heroism or unselfishness, or what seems so to us, we are struck by it. It seems a kind of forecast or prophecy of that higher moral life which we proudly thought was the monopoly of man. There is, then, vicarious sacrifice, but not that which makes such sacrifice *heroic*—the voluntary sacrifice of self for others, for their sake.

(2) But the moral appeal of an act of voluntary self-sacrifice increases with *the worth*

and greatness of the victim. And here, more than even in the willingness of the sacrifice, is seen the utter contrast between the law of nature and the law of love. By the law of nature the weak perish, the strong survive. The law is the "survival of the fittest." In the law of love all this is reversed. The strong bear the infirmities of the weak, the perfect suffer for the imperfect, the healthy for the diseased, the wise for the ignorant. It is this which gives strength to the appeal of what we call *heroism*. Why was it that only last year we were struck by the heroism of that young doctor[1] at the Bristol Infirmary, who sucked the poison from his patient's throat at the sacrifice of his own life? Take any estimate of value that you please, and that young doctor's life was worth far more than that of the poor creature he tried to save. Yet, in and through the loss of that brave life, we feel and know that humanity is the gainer, the richer for the act of self-forgetting devotion to duty. Why is it that when men dare to recommend to us the substitution of the natural for the moral, we resent it as an insult

---

[1] William Connor Lysaght, who died July 24, 1887. A memorial window has recently been placed in the Infirmary Chapel in commemoration of his death.

to our true nature? When, a little while ago, we were told by one[1] who posed as the champion of the "service of man," that the physically and morally diseased ought to be "suppressed," that the Christian teaching of repentance and forgiveness is hostile to morality, and that "medical skill and science have produced serious harm by saving weak and bad constitutions which would otherwise have perished;" or when a great biologist[2] protests against the tendency of modern philanthropy to promote "the survival of the unfittest;"—why do we feel ready with the indignant answer, "That may be science, but it is not morality, and we will not bring the law of love into conformity with that which, in the world outside us, our moral nature shudders at"? Why is it, again, that we feel it a gain when our best and noblest go out into the mission-field, to be the martyrs, perhaps, to a cruel climate, or at best to win to Christianity beings far lower than themselves? Is it not because, in all these cases, we recognize that which makes heroism what it is—the spirit of self-forgetfulness, which knows no law but the law of love, the giving

---

[1] "Service of Man," chs. v., ix.
[2] H. Spencer, "Man *versus* the State," p. 69.

of its best, and never stays to ask, "Is it worth while?"

If the Sacrifice of Jesus Christ stands alone in the unapproachableness of its moral beauty, no less than in the transcendent dignity and value of the Victim Who died, "the Just for the unjust," it is yet in line, if we may say so, with every act of self-denying love for others which appeals to the sympathy and to the hearts of men. The strength of its appeal is this—that for love of man, sinful and fallen though he was, the Eternal Word emptied Himself of His glory and took upon Him the servant's form, and humbled Himself to a degrading and painful Death. It was thus that He became the fulfilment of all those older sacrifices in which the innocent was given for the guilty, not only doing for man what those sacrifices could not do, but with the superadded power that His was a voluntary Death, a willing Sacrifice, so that He could say, as the forces of evil gathered round Him, and the shadows of Calvary deepened, and triumphant malice rejoiced over the Life so soon to be given over into its hands, "No man taketh it from Me, but I lay it down of Myself. I have power to lay it down, and I have power to take it again." "Greater love hath no man than this, that a man lay down his life for his friends."

The Death of Christ upon the Cross was the gathering up into one supreme moment of the manifold working of the law of love, which far back beyond the Christian ages had shown itself, as it shows itself still outside the circle of the faith of Christ, wherever man is man. And in every life which bears that impress of Christ's signet—self-forgetfulness, self-devotion, self-sacrifice—I seem to catch a gleam of brightness from the Cross of Jesus. It lights up every act of moral heroism, whether its scene is the battle-field, or the besieged city, or the more uneventful life of sympathy among the sick, or the suffering, or the sad. In the fever wards of the hospital, or amid the squalor and wretchedness of our great towns, or in the gentle tending of the little ones whom God leaves to the love of strangers, or in the loving hand held out to rescue the fallen and the lost; in all that we now vaguely call humanitarianism, no less than in the life sacrificed in defending or spreading abroad the truth of God, I see something which is Divine—superhuman, yet so intensely *human*—something which, consciously or unconsciously, draws from Calvary its inspiration and its power. For love, real love, is of God; nay, before the Cross of Christ we know it—*God is Love.*

But if the human appeal of an act of moral heroism reaches its climax when He Who offers Himself is the Eternal Son of God, it is lifted into a higher region when we remember the infinite reach of the love of God revealed in Christ. It is then that the appeal becomes a *claim.* " Greater love hath no man than this, that a man lay down his life for his friends." To the friends, at least, that death cannot be a mere appeal. It is a *claim.* Who were the " friends " for whom Christ died ? The soldiers who crucified, the unrighteous judge, the mocking multitude, the railing thieves, the Jews who rejected, ay, the traitor himself till he cast Christ's love away. Who are Christ's friends now whom from the Cross He claims? The world that resists Him to-day; the votaries of sin, of selfishness, of pleasure; the easy-going, comfortable man of the world; the passers-by to whom His Death is nothing but a memory or a regret. To all these, and to each one of us gathered before Him now, His love went forth from the Cross of suffering. To each He is speaking. He claims you. Will you not listen ? " I did all this for thee. What art thou doing for Me? My son, my daughter, give Me thine heart." "Not yours, but *you*,"—that is what Christ claims. "Remember," He seems to say again, "you are not your own; you are bought with a price. While you were yet sinners, I loved you, I died for you. I freed you from that 'clogging burden of a guilty soul' that you might be free to love Me—that in Me you might give yourselves a willing sacrifice, well pleasing unto God."

Do you not know that appeal, that claim, when it comes to you from some purely human source? Brothers, have you not heard it? Have you not felt its power? In the awful hour of strong temptation, when sinful passion came in like a flood, and opportunity for sin was ready, and the voice of prudence and the warnings of conscience were heard but in faint and feeble protest; when Reason seemed to totter on her throne, and the will no longer struggled to be free, have you never, in such a crisis as this, heard another voice— a voice which came straight from the memories of home, where the pure love of mother or of sister is enshrined; a voice "still and small," yet strong enough to claim you, and by its claim to check, as nothing else can, the rush of evil passion ; "still and small," yet loud enough to be heard above the roar and tumult and confusion ; "still and small," yet able to save you by its claim from that which would have been the regret, perhaps the misery, of a lifetime? And if human love has such power, what of the infinite love of Christ, our Elder Brother, Who is yearning over us with an undying love? There are lonely and solitary lives in this great crowded city, lives which feel themselves encompassed by no human sympathies, appealed to by no human heart, claimed by no human love; yet not one of these is outside the infinite love of Christ. His appeal is to them,—lost, wandering, outcast, neglected, sin-stained, defiled perhaps ; yet to them the appeal comes personal, direct, individual. Christ claims them for Himself. Oh! for the love of God, guard that precious truth of the world-wide reach of the love of God,—the world-wide efficacy of the Cross of Christ. If one soul is lost, it is because it has flung aside the appeal and claim of love, and said to Christ, "I will not have Thee." And, even to those who reject His love, He Who said, "I will draw all men unto Me," yet speaks in tones of pleading sadness, "Ye will not come unto Me, that ye might have life."

And not only in the hour of temptation, and to those who, but for the love of Christ, would be outcast and forsaken, but to each one of us in our ordinary life, the claim comes. What answer all our lives long have we been giving to Christ's appeal? What single thing is there in this past Lent that we have been doing just for the love of God? Ah! it is when we feel the claim of Christ's love that we learn for the first time all the miserable pettinesses of selfishness and pride; that we are able, nay, that we are constrained, to tear down all the thin disguises under which that self-love we thought we had triumphed over conceals its hated form; that we get a true standard for measuring what we once thought our great and noble acts, but which, in the light of Christ's love for us, seem limited, and mean, and poor, and worthless, and tawdry. We thought we were liberal, and self-denying, and humane, and charitable. Ah! but we have seen what love is as we rested for a minute before the Cross of Calvary; and as we go back to our busy, hurrying life it rings on with strange persistence in our ears,—"He laid down His life for us: and we ought to lay down our lives for the brethren." Yes, the claim of Christ's love is that, and nothing less—yourself, your whole self, and nothing but yourself. " Not yours, but you." Is there any other claim which can for one moment make good its appeal in rivalry with this? The noblest, holiest earthly love was but God's earthly messenger to win us back from baser things, and lead us back to that from which it came, the love of God. Brethren, is it a sacrifice, a surrender, when our heart feels itself claimed by that love? Is it not, rather, then only that love finds the object for which, in darkness and perplexity, it ever yearns, and realizes its one end? " We needs must love the highest when we see it;" and before the Cross we have seen the love of God.

"O Love, Who once in time wast slain,
  Pierced through and through with bitter woe !
   .   .   .   .   ,   .
  O Love, I give myself to Thee,
  Thine ever, only Thine to be."

III.

The Appeal to the Conscience and the Will.

THE Death of Christ upon the Cross comes to us with the *appeal* of moral heroism, and the *claim* of infinite love. It wins the homage of our emotions, our affections, our heart. But we distrust our emotions. It is not that we are ashamed to recognize the appeal of a noble act, or that we think it unmanly to admit the claim of love, but rather that we are jealous lest our emotions should betray us into a sacrifice of moral principle. "It is not the suffering, but the motive of the suffering," says S. Augustine "which makes the martyr." It is the end which distinguishes the true self-sacrifice of moral heroism from the fanaticism of self-immolation, and the cowardice of suicide. Our moral nature, then, wants to be reassured. It withholds its homage till conscience gives its judgment. The will can no more bow to that which is not right, than the heart can really love that which is not loveable. And those among us who are cast in the sterner mould, whose first thought is for the supremacy and integrity of the Moral Law, who even fear lest the pleasure which they feel in doing right, should detract from the purity of an act done for duty's sake, are specially sensitive and on their guard against that which appeals to their emotions. They fear lest emotional excitement should prove an anæsthetic of the conscience, and the will should be drawn aside from stern devotion to the law of right.

In regard to religious emotion especially, the conscience has learned a lesson of doubt, of caution, of distrust. It has seen too often the spectacle of religious enthusiasm which did not make for righteousness, of religious teachers who have put piety in place of moral purity, devotion instead of duty, nay, have misused the sacred claim of the love of God to dispense man from the love he owes his brother men. Conscience is right, then, to withhold its ready assent. Its office is to purify the emotional nature ; and to do so it must challenge it—put it, as it were, on its defence. Nor can conscience be satisfied with *à priori* arguments which might satisfy the heart. It might seem enough to say, "Shall not the Judge of all the earth do right?" Is it possible that the love of God can be other than just? Conscience cannot argue thus. It must be true to itself at all costs. It cannot recognize an appeal as from God till the moral test is satisfied. A being who claims to alter or dispense with the Moral Law, conscience boldly declares cannot be God.

Is, then, the love which from the Cross of Jesus appeals to and claims the love of man, able also to claim the recognition of our conscience, the allegiance of our will? Is Christ in His Life and Death the true moral Ideal for man as man? Is He "just" as well as "the Justifier of them that believe"?

(1) Of the verdict of conscience on the character of Christ, as that character is shown in His Life amongst men, we need not speak at length. Those who have been least willing to admit the Divinity of Christ have yet seen in Him the gathering up of all the highest moral aspirations of pre-Christian ages. The broken lights of heathen moral systems, no less than the progressive unfolding of the perfect character in the Law, the Prophets, and the Psalms, all find their unity, their

synthesis, in Him. But Christ does more than reveal to us the idea of humanity. In Him that idea lives and moves and has its being. "Ideas," says a great novelist,[1] "are often poor ghosts: our sun-filled eyes cannot discern them; they pass athwart us in their vapour, and cannot make themselves felt. But sometimes they are made flesh; they breathe upon us with warm breath; they touch us with soft responsive hands; they look at us with sad, sincere eyes, and speak to us in appealing tones; they are clothed in a living human soul, with all its conflicts, its faith, and its love. Then their presence is a power, then they shake us like a passion, and we are drawn after them with gentle compulsion, as flame is drawn to flame." It is not the revelation of an idea, but the realizing of an ideal in a perfect human life, which wins for the character of Christ the allegiance of the will.

(2) But it is with the Death of suffering which closed that perfect Life that we are specially concerned—with the mysterious work wrought on Calvary; the atonement made, the forgiveness won. What has conscience to say here? On the one hand, we are told that to pass over sin is immoral; on the other,

---

[1] Geo. Eliot, "Janet's Repentance," ch. xx.

that the immorality of letting off the sinner is increased by the punishment of the Sinless; in a word, that the doctrine of Substitution is a legal fiction, which shocks the conscience and insults man's moral nature.

Brethren, this protest of conscience is a true protest. Nowhere, as in its theory of the Atonement, has that false teaching of which I spoke done such deadly wrong to the appeal of God in Christ. Conscience, in rejecting that popular theory, passes a true judgment on the facts before it. But the facts are terribly, awfully falsified. (i.) God cannot pass over sin and treat it as if it were not. Conscience is right to demand the upholding of the Moral Law. A God who could ignore it could not be really God. (ii.) God cannot create or select a sinless man, and make him bear the punishment of sinners. "No man may deliver his brother, nor make atonement unto God for him." (iii.) Still less possible is it that the wrath of the Father should rest, for one moment, on the Well-Beloved Son, with Whom He is for ever One.

Conscience must judge the doctrine of the Atonement, not as explained away by those who have not realized what sin is, nor as travestied by popular Calvinism, nor as altered to fit a Unitarian creed, but as it is revealed in the Bible and the Church.

What is the demand of our moral nature? That God should uphold the Moral Law? Yes; but not that He should set the exaction of the penalty above that for which alone all penalties exist—the vindication of the law of righteousness. The deepest need of our moral nature is not to have the penalty remitted, but to be saved, delivered, from the sin. What does our moral nature demand? That God shall not pass over sin, or treat it as a little thing? Yes; yet no less clearly it demands, in God and man, a principle and power of forgiveness. It is these demands that are met by the doctrine of the Cross. What is its teaching? That God Himself, Who cannot even in thought be separated from the law of righteousness, has stooped, in love for man, to take humanity into Himself, and, as the Representative of human nature, has recognized and for ever vindicated by His Death the majesty and claim of the Moral Law.

Yes! conscience is right. God cannot pass over sin, and no legal fiction of substitution can satisfy our moral nature. But, in the presence of the Cross of Jesus, we bow before that which is not only a revelation of transcendent love, but an act of moral triumph. Before the Cross we see, as we see nowhere else, the deadliness of sin, and the majesty of that Law which sin has broken. Rather than that man made in God's image should perish, or the Moral Law remain unvindicated, He Who is Infinite Love will condescend to die that He may "save His people from their sins."

As, then, human love wins us back from baser things, and, half unconsciously, lifts us up to the source from which it flows; so conscience, with its imperious insistence on the Moral Law, reveals to us Him in Whom that Law abides, whose vicegerent conscience is. And we need no longer distrust emotions and affections which gather round the Person of Him, Whom conscience reverences as its Sovereign Lord, in Whose Life the moral ideal of humanity was realized, in Whose Death the eternal law of righteousness is vindicated and declared. The love of God in Christ, which claims our love, is no mere erotic thing. There is nothing of effeminacy in it. It has nothing in common with that weak, nerveless, immoral good-nature to which some in our day would seek to drag it down. It has in it an element of sternness, of severity, of jealous hatred of unrighteousness. It "can by no means clear the guilty." It cannot declare a general amnesty. It is irrevocably on the side of holiness. The truth that God cannot save a soul which puts sin in place of righteousness is no invention of Calvinism. It follows from the fact that God's love is a righteous love. Never to the ages of ages can God and sin exist side by side. They are separated for ever. The Atonement, because it is the vindication of the Moral Law, will profit them nothing who cast that Law aside. To love sin is to be separated from God; to love God is to be on the side of righteousness. "Ye that love the Lord, see that ye *hate* the thing that is evil." To feel the claim of the love of God is to have taken your stand irrevocably on the side of right.

Brethren, is that what the love of God means in your life? Have you felt its claim in your conscience and your will as the claim of Him, Whose Life was a moral victory, Whose Death was the Atonement for moral failure — the claim of the great Representative of human nature, by Whose power, though all unknowing, humanity in the past has won its noblest moral triumphs; Who gave to Joseph and to Scipio their chastity, to Regulus his stern devotion to duty, to Aristides his love of justice, to Codrus his willingness to die? Do you recognize it as the claim of One, Who on the Cross was Sponsor for you, and me, and all who in His strength will battle for the right; of One Who fulfilled the Law, not that we might be dispensed from it, but that we might fulfil it too, "being made the righteousness of God in Him;" of One Who now claims the offering of the wills which He has freed for willing service to a Holy God?

IV.

The Appeal to the Reason.

BEFORE the Cross we are in the presence of a great mystery—a mystery of Divine love, a mystery of moral triumph. It is the meeting-point of Heaven and earth. The love may claim and win our heart, the moral victory the allegiance of our will; but reason,—how can reason bow before a mystery? It owns no lord, no sovereign, but Truth. It must be true to itself. It must seek to *know*. Yet Christ claims the whole of human nature; not only the heart and the will, but the reason too, as His of right. He knows of no dualism in the nature He has taken into God; no separation between heart and will, or between moral and intellectual truth. He claims all because He *is* all. And the faith which is the answer to His claim is the faith that loves and wills and knows, and finds its perfect satisfaction in the manifested love of God.

But can the revelation of God from the Cross appeal to and claim the homage of our rational nature?

From two very different quarters a negative answer comes. There is—

(1) The answer of popular Calvinism. God's Will is supreme. His decrees are absolute. He has mercy on whom He will have mercy. Christ died for the elect. And who are they? The souls God chose, for no reason but in the absoluteness of free choice,—one here, one there. Bow your reason to God's Will, and recognize the mysteriousness of that selection. But do not ask, do not question, do not seek to know why, or you will be seeking for conditions, and so limiting God's power. Think rather of the omnipotence of One Who can pass over the noblest and purest, as we judge, and, of His mere will, single out from the mass of corruption a vessel made to honour. And this idea that we somehow magnify God by making His acts unintelligible, has laid hold of the imaginations of men who are far enough from Calvinism. They have come to think that it is rebellion to ask Why? and How? And so when, as in the present

day, reason tries to interpret the method of God's creation in the world of nature, in the light of what we see Him doing before our eyes, men are startled and shocked, as if it was inconsistent with God's power to work by law, by methods we can trace, or at least inconsistent with reverence for men to ask what those methods are. And yet reason is called upon to bow before this capricious, irrational, unintelligible, autocratic, arbitrary, tyrant-like God.

(2) Then there is the answer of the Agnostic. "You say reason has nothing to do with the matter. Be it so. Then reason will concern itself with that which it can deal with, and can know—with the orderly processes of nature. There is no caprice there, nothing which insults reason, or excludes reason. And as for that which claims to be lawless and irrational, we give it up to you. Believe it if you will, but do not call it 'knowable.' If reason has no place within your sacred precinct, neither has the revelation of your God any claim upon our reason."

It is plain that these two answers are correlative; the one is the obverse of the other. The one, indeed, seems reverent, the other defiant; yet both assume that God is not really "knowable" by man, and that the revelation of the Cross leaves reason unappealed to and unclaimed. The same false teaching which makes God's love selective, partial, limited,—human, not Divine,—which, by its teaching of predestination and denial of free-will, strikes at the root of our moral ideas,—also makes God irrational, and sets at defiance the reason which He gave to man. And, as the protest of the heart against a God Who is not Perfect Love, and of the conscience against Him Who is not Perfect Goodness, is a true protest, so the protest of the reason against an unknowable God is a true protest also.

For reason is right to own no sovereign but Truth. We talk about the submission of the reason, but reason would be wrong to submit to aught that is not true. There is no reasonable worship of an unknowable God. If reason offers its homage to what it can never know, it is false to itself, false to its duty to mankind, false to its mission from God. It must be true to itself. And it is true to itself when it questions, when it challenges, when it interrogates, when it theorizes, when it seeks to *know*. It is true to itself when it refuses to sacrifice one jot or tittle of fact to theory, and the intellectual pride which refuses to accept a truth is also intellectual impotence.

But reason is false to itself, when it loses reverence and earnestness, and puts away with a smile of incredulity facts which it cannot yet explain, or gives less weight to these than to those which fit its theory. Reason is false to itself, when it settles down contented to ignore what it cannot by its present methods adequately interpret. Reason is false to itself when, in the presence of that which for eighteen centuries has been one of the greatest motive-powers in the world, and which still stirs the heart and conscience as nothing else can, it is willing to say, "It is outside my province; I know it not." Reason is false to itself when it contemplates unmoved the atrophy of one side of human nature, and sacrifices the whole to the fragment. Reason is, above all, false to itself when it settles a question which it has not cared to examine, and takes it for granted that God cannot be known.

Why is it that reason, with all its magnificent triumphs in the domain of nature, is so powerless in dealing with the facts of man's moral and spiritual nature; that it shirks the problem, or explains away the facts, or declares that they belong to faith or feeling, as though these were not things of which reason must give account? It is not *mystery* that reason rebels at. For mystery lies behind all we know. It is the background of the knowledge we have won, the stimulus to the knowledge we have yet to gain. It is not *difficulty* which reason shrinks from. It does not shrink from difficulties elsewhere. It expects, it welcomes, it exults in them, as a brave man exults in danger. What reason rebels at is that which excludes reason—the irrational, the lawless, the capricious. And when men talked of a capricious God, a God Whose absoluteness could not conceal His arbitrariness, reason was excluded from the sacred courts. And after a little struggle it acquiesced in the exclusion, and as a consequence has become " cabin'd, cribb'd, confined " in the region of sensible fact. And at last, like a slave who hugs his chains, it exults in its own impotence. Then we hear such words as these, " I have swept the heavens with my telescope and I have seen no God." Therefore God is not, or He cannot be known by man. " I have dissected many a human body," says another, " but my scalpel has never brought to light a soul." Therefore religion is meaningless. I see no place in the physical system, says another, for what men call moral freedom. Banish it, then; it is a "current illusion,"[1] and responsibility is a name we have coined to justify us in finding fault.[2]

And this blandly dogmatic negation, this *à priori* theorizing about unexamined facts, this calm reassertion in the conclusion of an assumption made in the premiss, has usurped the place of reason.

But why has reason thus become false to itself in moral and spiritual matters, while it is so true in the world of nature? As long as nature was thought of as a chaos of warring wills, reason was powerless there; it ceased to investigate, to interrogate, to verify. But when it threw itself upon nature, and made its "act of faith," and assumed that nature was a "cosmos" from end to end, dominated throughout by the reign of law, then it felt the claim of nature, which is the claim of God, and entered on its triumphant course. And so long as we religious teachers allow ourselves to think and speak of God as lawless and

---

[1] H. Spencer, "Psychology," vol. i., p. 500.
[2] "What do we gain by this fine language as to moral responsibility? The right to blame, and so forth."—"Service of Man," p. 293.

irrational, and banish reason from the area of religion, we cannot blame reason if it abandons the religious problem, and treats it as insoluble.

The Church, then, has its own "act of reparation" to make to God. It must welcome reason once more to its heart, if it is to be the true home of thinking men. And reason has its "act of faith" to make here as in the field of nature, if it is to realize and interpret those facts of the heart and conscience, of which the Cross of Christ is at once the centre and the key.

It was Calvinism begat Agnosticism. In the beginning it was not so. *Christ* never slights the reason which He gave when man was created "in the image of God." He never calls on it to bow to anything but truth. He appeals to it, He claims it, because He is the Truth and the Revealer to man of a "knowable" God. "I am the Way, the Truth, and the Life: no man cometh unto the Father, but by Me;" "Ye shall know the truth, and the truth shall make you free." *S. Paul* did not distrust reason. He appealed to it and claimed it, when he summoned men from the irrational worship of an unknown God to the knowledge of the Father revealed in Christ. Again and again he summons intellectual men from the wisdom of the world, which was no wisdom, to the knowledge of the truth. He himself was ever "following on to know the Lord." His ideal was "to know Christ and the power of His Resurrection," "to know the things which are freely given us of God." Even in the great mystery of Holy Communion, he appeals fearlessly to reason. "I speak as to wise men; judge ye what I say. The Cup of blessing which we bless, is it not the Communion of the Blood of Christ?" The *Church of the Fathers* did not fear reason. They claimed it, as S. Paul had done, on the side of the Cross. In S. Clement, in S. Athanasius, in S. Augustine, reason finds its noblest exercise within the sacred area of revelation. It is at home there, no less than in the region of the natural. It was heretical only when it was false to itself, and denied the facts which it could not explain. The mediæval Church did not fear reason. Here still reason lived and wrought and dared to speculate on the deepest mysteries of God; nay, as the great schoolman, our own S. Anselm, reminds us, men felt it to be a duty to make faith rational, no less than to believe.[1] The speculations of mediæval

---

[1] "Cur Deus Homo?" *sub init.*

thinkers are not ours. We cannot understand why reason should have been so active in the sphere of religion, and be atrophied in the region of nature. But their teaching is still true, that, in revelation and nature too, faith is the door of rational knowledge. And when faith was strong, the Church bid her children *believe* in order that they might *know;* when faith grew weak, false teachers said, *Believe*, but do not try to *know*. And soon reason, which could not but strive for knowledge, came to think itself the enemy of faith, and was driven to seek its object away from God.

Brethren, God speaks to you from the Cross as reasonable men, and claims your reason—claims it as His of right; for He is Truth. The mystery of the Cross is also a revelation of a knowable God. You resent, and resent rightly, that which insults reason—the irrational, the arbitrary, the capricious, the meaningless, the wayward. Is there anything of this in God, in nature, or in man? Not in *God;* for God is Love. There are no episodes or accidents in the life of God. All is calm, majestic order; all is firm, unswerving purpose. Not in *nature;* for there, in ever-growing clearness, we trace the reflex of God's being in the reign of law—the firm and stately march of unfolding life. But in *man*,—yes, in man there is disorder, confusion, loss of harmony, frantic, lawless movement. For in man there is *sin*. And sin is the enemy of order, of law, of God. It is not free-will which disturbs the order of the world. God's Will is free; but there is no variableness in Him, no shadow of turning. God's freedom is the necessity of doing right. No; it is not free-will, but the false freedom of self-will, which, like the freedom of a locomotive which has left the metals, is the freedom of destruction, and self-destruction. And men exulted in self-will, and then made God in their own likeness, and thought of Him as lawless. And all the time He was seeking to restore them to the image of Himself. And all the revelation of God in conscience, in the Bible, in the Church, all the world of miracle and supernatural power which seems to break in upon the reign of law, even the mystery of the Incarnation and the Atonement, are integrated parts of the great purpose to win back man from lawlessness to order, from sin to God.

Yes, the Cross appeals to man's reason no less than to his heart and will; claims him on the side of order and of law and truth. How long, O Lord, shall reason resist or fail to recognize that claim? It cannot be but that man shall some day be true to himself. It cannot be but that a day shall come when reason, that strong giant which cannot worship and will not pray, shall know that, in its earnest love of truth, it bore upon its shoulders, as in the ancient legend, the Saviour of the world. It cannot be but that a day shall dawn—

> "When Faith shall grow a man, and Thought a child,
> And that in us which thinks with that which feels
> Shall everlastingly be reconciled,
> And that which questioneth with that which kneels."

The Words from the Cross.

The Words from the Cross.

Introduction.

WE are here to-day, not to listen to sermons, but to see God; to hear Him speaking to our souls; to recognize, if He will, more than ever we have done before, the appeal of Christ to our whole nature, His claim upon our heart, our conscience, and our reason. We have come to open our hearts to the love of God, and let that love, in all its rich fulness, transform us into itself. And in order to do this, we are going to be for a little while—only a part, perhaps, of these solemn three hours—alone with God, alone in this great congregation, for God will speak to each soul in the language that it knows, in tones which vibrate in the memory, as from One Who knows our inner history.

We have come apart, brethren, to spend a

little while at the foot of the Cross. We have put away our duties, our business, our pleasure. We have exchanged the brightness of this fair spring morning for the dark church, and the sombre service, and the Cross of suffering. We have come to recall the well-known scene just that, in and through it, God may teach us more about Himself, and about His love.

But if we are to see God, something more is needed. We must not only come apart from the world; we must separate ourselves from the circle of its ideas. We must forget what the world thinks God ought to be, and see Him as He is, as He reveals Himself.

Moses, the representative of the Law, Elijah, the representative of the Prophets, who saw Christ on the Transfiguration Mount, had both, in their earthly life, received a revelation from God, and it was strangely different from what they hoped to see. Moses longed to be assured that God was with him, and as a sign he asked, " I beseech Thee shew me Thy Glory." And the answer comes, " I will make all My goodness pass before thee." And, hidden in the clift of the rock, he heard those wonderful words, " The Lord, the Lord God, merciful and gracious, long-suffering, and abundant in goodness and truth."

Not otherwise was it with Elijah. God had wrought a great miracle on Carmel, and men were not converted; and the Prophet, in disappointment and weariness, longs to die. And in Horeb God revealed Himself. The mighty wind, the earthquake, the fire, passed—the Lord was not in them; but in the "still small voice" the Prophet recognized the Presence of God.

So with us to-day. We must look for God's revelation, not in power, but in love; not in excitement or violent emotion, but in some still small voice, with its message of warning, or of pardon, or of goodness. Men look for some mighty, overmastering, irresistible force; and God's method is to appeal to,—to claim,—to win.

We want, then, our Blessed Lord to-day to tell us about Himself, and about ourselves; just to say to us that word, we know not what it is, that our souls long to know, which may make us His—just a word straight from the Cross which will transform our life, or deepen our love, or enlarge our knowledge, or mould our will. We want at least to go to our homes different somehow from what we were when we came here. Perhaps we did not think much what we came for. Perhaps what we want most is to know what we do want. Some of us, no doubt, do know quite clearly what we want most. We want deliverance from some great haunting memory, which is ever coming between us and God; or we want guidance in our life and work; or we want—which of us does not?—more light in the weary problems that beat, and baffle us, and hinder our Christian life. And sometimes we are so anxious to blurt out all our wants to God that His voice is drowned in our prayers. Sometimes we are quite wrong as to the real need of our souls, and so cannot understand His Word, when it is different from what we expect. To learn how to learn is sometimes a hard lesson, because it means letting God teach.

We are going to listen to the words from the Cross. And it can't be wrong or artificial to seek to trace in them something of an order and a sequence. We treasure up the last words of a dying friend not only because they are the last, but because they seem to reveal to us something of what is going on in the soul about to pass through the waters of death. So these last words of our Lord are precious to us, because they tell us all that we may dare to know, all that He has willed to reveal, of His last thoughts in His agony.

A long interval of silence and darkness seems to have separated the first three and the last four words, and there is a corresponding difference of character in the words themselves. In the first three, Christ speaks to man; in the last four, the Son holds mysterious converse with the Father. In the first three, the love of God looks down upon the types of men who were present at the Cross. The Divine love prays for the unrepentant world, the crucifiers, the crowd, the indifferent passers-by: "Father, forgive them." It is the word of intercession. The Divine love turns to the poor penitent upon the Cross. For him it has a message of forgiveness: "This day shalt thou be with Me in Paradise." It is the word of absolution. The Divine love looks down in tender care upon the faithful ones beneath the Cross: "Behold thy son; behold thy mother." It is the word of blessing. Then the darkness gathers and deepens, and nature is wrapped in gloom till the supreme moment when the Perfect Man, bearing the curse of sin that is not His own, cries aloud to the Father, and we hear those other words which tell of the separation, the longing, the triumph, and the rest in God. But it was love all through. It was love that prayed, and love that pardoned, and love that blessed, and love that bore the curse, and love that yearned, and love that triumphed, and love that entered on its Sabbath rest.

This is the revelation of love which Christ holds out to us to-day. This is the love which claims us as its own.

I.—The Priest in Intercession.

"Father, forgive them; for they know not what they do."—
S. Luke xxiii. 34.

"Father, forgive them!" It is the first time the Crucified has spoken. Perhaps it was while the cruel nails were driven home, or while the transverse bar, with its living burden, was being raised into its place. We do not know; only we are sure it was not only for the men who with cruelty or carelessness, perhaps, were but obeying orders, that the Sufferer prayed when "He made intercession for the transgressors." It was for the crowd who mocked, and the soldiers who amused themselves, and the priests who avenged the insult passed on their Messianic hope, by disowning with taunt and jeer "the King of the Jews;" and Pilate, the unrighteous judge, who had pleased the people at the cost of his conscience; and Herod, the puppet-king, who had played his part in the hollow pageant and the mock trial of a supposed rival;—for all these, aye, and for you and me, and all who in these eighteen centuries have disowned, or passed by, or rejected, or scorned, or sold for money, or frustrated by open or secret sin the love of God. "Father, forgive them!" How unlike our prayers! How different from our charity, which begins at home and mostly stays there! Christ's love begins at a point we hardly ever reach. It thinks of its enemies first.

"Father, forgive them!" For the rejection of the Son is treason against the Father Himself. "No man cometh unto the Father, but by Me." And "he that hateth Me, hateth My Father also." "Father, forgive them" who in this day receive not the revelation Thou hast given from the Cross of Jesus. Truly, "they know not what they do." They cannot have seen that love as we have seen it, and yet reject its claim. Does not the Unitarian love God? Does not the theist love God? Surely they do not know. They are jealous for the honour due to the Eternal Father, and so they will not bow before the Divine Son, in Whom the Father is revealed; or they are staggered by some false theory of the Atonement; or they are anxious, with a charity which seems as if it must come from the God of love, to claim for God those who are living noble lives, and are not Christian;—and so they try, in some modern Arian belief, to find a middle term between Christianity and natural religion. At least, while the Saviour's prayer is in our ears, and the love which believeth all things and hopeth all things is in our hearts, we must hold as long as we can that defiant unbelief, in men of pure and loving lives, is very, very rare. And yet we join in the prayer of Christ, " Father, forgive them; they know not what they do." They know not that, in rejecting the faith of Christ, they are destroying that very belief in the Father which they value most. Surely faith in God, in our day, is indissolubly bound up with the truth of Christianity. They who in these days can stand upon the razor-edge of theism, with a pantheism on one side which destroys personality, and a materialism on the other which denies God, are few and far between.

"Father, forgive them!" Deep in the heart of the Church was treasured up that lesson from the Cross. "Lord, lay not this sin to their charge!" cried the first martyr, S. Stephen, as he thought upon the King of Martyrs. "O Lord," cried S. James, the Bishop of Jerusalem, when he was thrown from the battlements of the Temple, and lay almost dead—"O Lord, pardon them; for they know not what they do!" Again and again has the Christian martyr raised Christ's prayer of intercession, as he remembered his Lord. The greatest proof that the Church had drunk in the spirit of this word of Christ's is that they not only forgave, but were able to make excuse. Listen to S. Peter, the loving, impetuous, impulsive disciple; surely he will raise no plea for those who killed his Lord. Yet, speaking to them, he says, "Brethren, I wot that through ignorance ye did it, as did also your rulers." Even S. Peter had learned that lesson from the Cross. Listen to S. Paul, again, who once had crucified Christ in His followers, but obtained mercy because he did it ignorantly —listen to him as he tells the Corinthians of the wisdom which this world's princes knew not, for "had they known it they would not have crucified the Lord of Glory." Yes, the Church had learned the lesson of forgiveness, of love to enemies, of willingness to make excuse.

What a hard lesson it is to learn! It implies so much love, so much self-forgetfulness. And pain, whether bodily or mental, is so selfish, so exclusive, so absorbing. Think of some time when you were in pain, suffering just from some ordinary pain—a bad headache, perhaps, or some ordinary worry. What happened? Duties were neglected, prayers limited; we could think of nothing; we could not bear people near us; we were irritable, and fancied every one must know that we were suffering. Women bear pain better than men because as a rule they are more unselfish. For most of us men, in spite of our boasted strength, it needs nothing but a little pain to bring out all the selfishness in us. But our Lord, in all the torture of body and distress of soul, thinks first of others, and those others the very men who had caused His pain. "Father, forgive them," the crucifiers! Dear friends, is there any one who has wronged you? Carry his name before God. You can pray for one you hate, you cannot hate one you pray for.

And if we ever get so far as really to forgive, it is often such a poor self-seeking forgiveness after all. We are so proud of the Christian spirit we have shown, that we magnify the wrong done us so as to increase our goodness in forgiving it. It is so much easier to forgive than to make excuse for others, to persuade ourselves that we have nothing to forgive, that the wrong done was not meant, or that the wrong-doer did not know. The very suggestion hurts our pride. And so we go and talk it over with a neighbour and compare notes, and come back quite sure the wrong was meant, and if we forgive it it is real Christian charity. But Christ's love pleads to the Father for the crucifiers because they did not know.

Did they not know, the crucifiers? And if not, why did they need forgiveness? Ah! you cannot apply those sharp divisions to the mysterious fact of sin. It is part of the very irrationality of sin that the sinner knows, and yet he knows not. No one chooses evil for evil's sake. Yet there is no sin without a known resistance of conscience. Pilate did not know that he had sentenced to death the Judge of all the earth; but he knew that he had condemned an innocent Man. The Jews did not know they were crucifying their Messiah; but they knew that for envy, and not for justice, they had delivered Him to Pilate. So do we never know the full meaning of our acts. The evil word is spoken: we know it is wrong: but we did not know its finished work would be the defiling and the ruin of some virgin soul. The half-meant sneer is uttered: we knew it was wrong: but we did not know that, like a cold east wind, it would blight the tender growth of a brother's faith. Do young men know when they go near temptation, or when they play with unbelief, the bitter cry of penitence or hopelessness which will some day rise to God? Does a father know what he is doing when he sends his son to church and stays away himself, or the mother when she is so busy that she leaves to others that most sacred duty of teaching her children the love of God?

Brethren, as you pray for forgiveness think of your secret faults. May it not be that the Saviour's prayer is bringing home to you something you never thought of as a sin, which, now you know it, makes you throw yourself before the Crucified with the prayer, " Forgive me, Lord; I knew not what I did"?

II.—The Priest in Absolution.

"This day shalt thou be with Me in Paradise."—
S. Luke xxiii. 43.

"This day shalt thou be with Me in Paradise." It is the word of pardon. Divine love, which sought first the unrepentant world, now turns its gaze upon the penitent, the firstfruits of the Saviour's prayer, the first to receive the forgiveness He has won. The Priest in intercession becomes the Priest in absolution.

"And with Him they crucify two thieves." In their last agony those sinful men are brought into the Presence of the Sinless One. And sin hates holiness. What wonder that in their pain they reviled the Christ!

But the majesty of that silent suffering and the love of that interceding prayer has touched the heart of one of them, and awed him into silence. As the darkness gathers round, his voice is no longer heard reviling. Who can say what was passing in that soul? How long will the power of sin struggle against the Saviour's prayer? That rough, violent man, if such he was, his hands red with crime, was one who "knew not what he did." The Saviour's prayer had included him. And the light is breaking on his soul—the light of self-knowledge—and the contrast between himself, the criminal, and the sinless Christ forces itself home. It is only in the Presence of the All-Holy, that we see the blackness of sin. And to be conscious of sin is the first step towards confession. He cannot be silent now. "Dost not thou fear God?" What a strange question for one criminal to ask another! Is not our punishment just? Is not His unjust? "We receive the due reward of our deeds." What a strange recognition of the majesty of the Moral Law, from one who had so lately joined in the railings! A confession made upon a cross! Yes, he has withdrawn by silence from the mocking crowd. He has broken with his comrade by that stern rebuke. He has made his confession to Almighty God; and now he commits himself unreservedly, with all the dark stain of sin upon him, unto the mercy of God. "Lord, remember me when Thou comest into Thy kingdom." And in a moment the answer comes, "This day shalt thou be with Me in Paradise."

Dear friends, there is in that word comfort for the penitent and for those of troubled heart. Do not suffer yourselves, in fear of that false and dangerous teaching which gathers round what some call "the doctrine of assurance," to let slip the precious truth of the entire absolution of the penitent. "This day." There is nothing of doubt or uncertainty here, no delay interposed, no period of probation ordered. And that present certainty of pardon is what the penitent longs for; not exemption from the penalty—the dying thief suffered that to the last degree; not a light-hearted forgetfulness of sin—that is impossible for a real penitent—but just the knowledge that he is once more in the grace of God; that the channels of communication which sin had clogged are opened anew, that he is enfolded in the love of God, that he has found peace. That is the gift the Saviour gave to the dying thief. That is the gift He is ready to give now to every penitent soul. Yet there are many whom God would have to be at peace, who are disquieting themselves in vain, and marring their spiritual growth, because they cannot know that they are safe. They are seeking for that knowledge in themselves, and yet they dare not trust themselves. Surely it was not in vain that He Who knows us best gave "power and commandment to His ministers" to declare to the penitent the absolution of his sins, nor is it in vain that those words are said to every priest at his Ordination, "Whose sins thou dost forgive, they are forgiven," nor is it in vain that he is bidden to say at the bedside of the dying penitent, "By Christ's authority committed to me, I absolve thee from all thy sins, in the Name of the Father, and of the Son, and of the Holy Ghost."

Does it seem strange that the sins of a life, a long resistance of God's grace, should be pardoned thus, and one act of penitence, one look of faith, should be met by an answer of peace? The acts of Christ's love are always strange to us. It is so unlike what we should have done to think first of our crucifiers, and pray for them. It is so unlike the way we should deal with a penitent, to receive him to our heart at once. It could not be, if it were not that every act of faith, every cry of penitence, is an answer to the Saviour's prayer, makes possible the Saviour's absolution.

I have read a legend of the days when saints were believed to visit our earth, and it tells how a saint as he went through a great city with a holy monk was met by a man who was living a life of open sin. I know not whether it was the brightness of a Divine purity that dazzled the sinner's eye, or whether the saint's glance reflected something of the love of Calvary; but in a moment that man who had not bowed his knee in prayer for thirty years threw himself at the saint's feet, and raised the prayer of penitence to God, "Lord, save me—save me from myself!" The monk, angry that the sinner should come near the saint, rebukes him, and in self-righteous wrath utters aloud the prayer, "Lord, grant that in the judgment-day I may be far from sinners such as he." Then the saint spoke. "Two prayers have risen to God, and both are heard. Poor penitent, the love of God has wrapped thee round. The Saviour's prayer is heard. In the great day of God thou shalt be near the throne: and thou, self-righteous monk, shalt have thy wish; thou shalt be far from him." Such is the signal honour God sets on penitence.

Oh! Christ is praying for many here who know not what they do when they resist His love. You have come here, some of you, perhaps, almost by chance. It was a holiday, and you wanted to see the cathedral during a service, and you did not know that God's love was drawing you, calling you to look Him in the face, to hear His intercession for you. And now He is waiting to follow up the word of intercession with the word of absolution. "To-day"—He is waiting for what? Just for that which the thief offered on the cross—it was all he had; it is all we have—the confession of sin, the prayer of faith.

Lord, remember me. I am sin-stained, defiled. I did not know what I was doing. I did not know that prayer was being raised for me. I was made in God's image. Remember not my sins, but remember me. Say to my soul that word of absolution, "To-day shalt thou be with Me."

"In Paradise," the ante-chamber of Heaven, the garden of delights about the palace of God, or in this heaving, toiling, restless world, what matters it so long as I am with Thee? "In Thy Presence there is the fulness of joy; at Thy right hand there are pleasures for evermore."

III.—The Priest in Blessing.

"Woman, behold thy son! . . . Behold thy mother."—
S. John xix. 26, 27.

The Priest from the altar of the Cross has made His intercessory prayer for the sinful world; He has spoken the word of pardon to the penitent thief. He has yet another act of goodness in store: He has a word of tenderness and blessing for those who stand "faithful among the faithless" at the foot of the Cross.

And who are they? Three women and one man. Of the chosen twelve one had betrayed, and one had denied, and all had fled, and only one had dared to return and seek his Master at the Cross. Oh, how the love of those brave women puts our cowardice to shame! Theirs is a love which does not reason, it endures and waits; it does not calculate, it simply clings—clings with a grasp which is stronger than death, for it draws its power from the Perfect Love.

For two of that little group the Priest upon the Cross has a special blessing. What reward shall be given to such persistent, all-enduring love? Perhaps if those sad ones could have been asked they would have said, "Oh! give us death. The brightness is gone out of our lives. Earth cannot be to us what it has been. All that is dearest is taken from us. Let us but pass into the waiting world, where the wicked cease from troubling, and the weary are at rest." And if that prayer had been granted they would not have known the joy of the Easter morning, or the calm and tender love of that new relationship which began at the Cross.

Lady, "behold thy son." Faithful friend, "behold thy mother." The whispered words are caught by loving ears. "And from that hour that disciple took her unto his own home." That word from the Cross has given a new relationship, has sanctified and transformed a tender earthly love.

So does Christ lift into a higher region all that is deepest and truest in earthly affections. Yet often it seems to be the sundering of earthly ties, and the blighting of earthly hopes. Why is this? Christ would win us wholly. And "he that loveth son or daughter more than Me is not worthy of Me." And so the sword must pierce that Mother's heart. The natural affection so exclusive, so almost selfish, must bear to see the Divine Son doing

His Father's Will upon the Cross, as once He left His earthly home to be "in His Father's house." But He will not leave the Mother comfortless. "Behold thy son; behold thy mother." And the Holy Virgin-mother and the well-beloved disciple are now bound each to each by a supernatural bond. They have found one another in Him they lost. "From that hour that disciple took her unto his own home."

It was natural, we say, that those two loving hearts should be drawn together. Who so fitting to comfort her, on whose breast once the infant Saviour lay, as that loved friend who lay in Jesus' bosom? Would not the Mother's love go out to him who had drunk so deeply of the love of Christ? Would not the disciple cling to her, the Mother of his Lord? Yes, it was natural. And because it was natural, Christ gave it His Priestly blessing, and made the natural love a sacred tie.

Does not Christ do the same still, lifting the natural love into a supernatural life? What of holy marriage and those other relationships over which marriage throws its shield? Is not the union of man and woman natural? Yes, but Christian marriage is a

F

supernatural thing, a sacred mystery from first to last. As in that first miracle at the marriage feast, the presence of Christ turns the water of natural affection into the wine of a sacred love. "What God hath joined together, let not man put asunder." Dear people, we have come apart from the world, its tumults and its strifes, to be alone before the Cross of Jesus. But soon we must return to that world again to act our part for God. What have we learned at the Cross? Two views of marriage are before the world now: the natural and legal on the one side, the supernatural and the Christian on the other. Christ claims to have sanctified and transformed the natural union, and to have created the marriage law of Christendom. And in this nineteenth century you are called upon to say whether the supernatural tie is real, and whether it can touch with its own supernaturalness relationships which are not of blood. Is Christian marriage an act in which the ever-present Priest lifts up the natural into the Divine life, giving to husband and wife a new relationship to one another, and to one another's kin; or is it a natural union of two wills, round which a halo of religiousness has grown? Surely "they know not what they do" who would abandon the outworks of Christian marriage and still hold the citadel. All experience is against it. Christians! will you dare to fight for the "scientific frontier" Christ has won from the natural life?

And then what of the love of parents for their children? Isn't it natural? Isn't it, as we say, an instinct, having its counterpart throughout the animal world? Ah! fathers and mothers, yours must be a higher love than this. You must learn that hard lesson (doesn't it come from the Cross?)—must learn to give your dear ones up, to work for God perhaps away from you, or to rest with Him in the waiting world, and yet to know that they are only really yours when they are wholly His.

And so with all those natural ties which bind man to man in friendship or in love. They are beautiful wild flowers which Christ transplants into the garden of God. Isn't the home a natural sphere of love? Isn't the State a natural growth? Isn't the love of country a true instinct? Yet Christ would lift all these into a supernatural region, the family of God, the Divine society, the "city which hath foundations."

So, too, Christ claims and consecrates all that is most generous in our natural impulses. But the change from the natural to the supernatural must be wrought before the Cross. Perhaps a great crushing sorrow comes. Life seems broken off short. Is it worth living? Darkness is all round; and down through the darkness there comes a message from the Cross which opens up to us a new life, a new work for God. I have read of one, a brave young Spanish knight, in the days of chivalry, one whose first thought was to make a name by deeds of arms, and lay his laurels at the feet of the lady of his love. His glorious career was cut short by a terrible wound. He was a cripple for life. All his bright hopes were shattered; months of suffering and pain were before him, and then what? What had God in store for that brave life on which, so young, the shadow of the Cross had fallen? Wonderfully God led him on. In prayer and self-examination the change was wrought. In a lonely monastery he hung up his knightly weapons, in the rough garment of penitence he went forth to work for God: his General, Christ,—the Lady to whom all his chivalrous love was now transferred, the Mother of the Lord,—he went forth to fight for God. The world knows him as the captain of the great Church army of Rome in the sixteenth century—Ignatius de Loyola.

Are there not sad lives here to-day?—lives broken off, weary, useless?—lives that see nothing but the darkness, and have not heard the word from the Cross, giving them a new charge, a new work for God? Christ is waiting to consecrate those sorrowing lives, and make them strong, by a word from the Cross.

IV.—THE SEPARATION.

"My God, My God, why hast Thou forsaken Me?"—
S. Matt. xxvii. 46.

A long silence separated the third from the fourth word. "From the sixth hour there was darkness over all the land unto the ninth hour. And about the ninth hour Jesus cried with a loud voice, saying, My God, My God, why hast Thou forsaken Me?"

Before the darkness had gathered, the Crucified, in all His pain, had looked down from the Cross, had prayed for the sinners, had pardoned the penitent, had blessed the faithful. But on the altar of the Cross Christ is Himself the Sacrifice—

> "Offered was He for greatest and for least,
> Himself the Victim and Himself the Priest."

And it seems as if in this second act, as it were, of the Divine drama, between the ninth hour and the moment of death, we can trace step by step the work of the great Atonement. He was made sin for us though He knew no sin, that we might be made the righteousness of God in Him. It was the fulfilling of the Divine purpose of the Incarnation when "God was made man that man might be made God." In Christ crucified, human nature died to sin that it might live unto God, and each individual soul that passes from death to life must tread in Christ the *via crucis*—must know the pain of separation and the longing for God, before it tastes the joy of triumph and can rest in Him.

> "O generous love! that He Who smote
> In man for man the foe,
> The double agony in man
> For man should undergo,
> And in the garden secretly,
> And on the Cross on high,
> Should teach His brethren and inspire
> To suffer and to die."

What did it mean, that great and bitter cry of separation? It was the very climax of the sufferings of Christ. How shall we speak of it? Like the darkness which was its external sign, we may say what it was not. That pall of darkness surely was no natural eclipse; but in some strange way nature, which is gathered up in man, showed its sympathy with the Perfect Man, Who in the only real sense is the Lord of nature. And the separation which that darkness symbolized, what was it? Again, we know what it was not. It was not a separation between the Father and the Son. They are for ever one in love and will and being. It was not the separation of the Divine and human natures in our Lord. That could not be without undoing the work of the Incarnation. But in some mysterious way Christ felt the desolating weight of sin. "His but not His." "For the Lord hath laid on Him the iniquity of us all." How infinitely greater the suffering implied in that cry of loneliness than in all the body's pain! "Pain of body," it has been said, "is but the body of pain; the soul of pain is the pain, the suffering of the soul." "My God, My God, why hast Thou forsaken Me?" When Christ stood by the grave of Lazarus, He, the Resurrection and the Life, in presence of death had prayed, "Father, I thank Thee that Thou hast heard Me. And I knew that

Thou hearest Me always." Even when He had foreseen the desertion of His dearest earthly friends, the knowledge that the Father was with Him was His comfort. "Ye shall be scattered, and leave Me alone; and yet I am not alone, because the Father is with Me." Now it is no longer "Father," for He speaks as the Sin-bearer, and humanity in Him under the curse of sin cries out in agony to God. "Not alone," yet "forsaken." What is this?

I suppose when we read that Christ was in all points made like unto His brethren, sin only excepted, we have all sometimes thought, "Yes, and just because He could not sin, He never could have known that desolating sense of separation which the sinner feels in the presence of God. I think I could bear anything if I knew that God's smile was resting on me—suffering, yes, suffering and even death, if I felt beneath me the everlasting arms, and above me the hand of God." Yet Christ did know that desolation, though He knew no sin, and it was the supreme moment of His agony when He tasted the cup of loneliness for us.

Why is it we can enter so little into this loneliness of Christ? Oh, brethren, sin is around us, and about us, and within us. We live in it, we move in it as an atmosphere, we take it as a matter of course. We do not realize its foulness, its hideousness, its hateful deformity. If for one moment we could see it as God sees it, we should shriek with horror, we should fly from it. Even if just for a little moment, in the presence of God, we catch a glimpse of sin as it is, how we loathe and hate and despise it! How utterly alien it is from God, from all that we really love! Oh! men do not know when they touch sin and play with defilement. They know not what they do. But Christ knew sin, saw it as it was, in all its creeping loathesomeness; and that foul thing He took upon Himself for love of us. He lifted it into His arms, He bore it on His shoulders. He was clothed with it, and yet He was Very God and Perfect Holiness. Have you ever for one moment felt the shuddering horror of defilement? Have you ever seen sin? Think, then, what must have been the agony of Christ when He, the Sinless One, was wrapped round with the sins of others, and cried aloud, "My God, My God, why hast Thou forsaken Me?" "Forsaken," "not alone."

Brethren, that agony in the touch of sin is

bound up with a real knowledge of God. You do not know sin till you know God, and see in sin the great separator. Men talk about the pains of hell. Surely, if the lost soul could by a miracle be carried across the great gulf he would carry his hell with him; nay, perhaps hell is hell, only because the sinner is in the presence of God, and knows himself separated from Him. God grant that you and I may know God here, may feel the awful desolating power of sin while the day of salvation lasts, and we may throw ourselves on the mercy of God. Anything rather than that we should live the painless life of those who live in sin and never hate it, over whom the yearning Love looks down in helpless sorrow. For they are "dead while they live."

But if we have felt, or are feeling, however little, what it is to be separated from God by sin, there is a word of comfort out from the thick darkness of the Cross: "Forsaken," "not alone." The separation of the soul from God cannot be absolute while it is able to cry, "My God." "My God," though now Thou art far off and seemest to hide Thy face. "My God," for Thou wilt never leave me nor forsake me. Thou hast made me for Thyself. With all the memory of defiling sin, and the darkness of the curse between, my soul yet reaches upwards in the cry, "My God."

"Not alone," yet "forsaken." In the solemn hour of dying, it will sometimes happen even to God's children—nay, perhaps the more because they are His children and know what sin is—that the consciousness of the old sins, repented of and pardoned though they be, will seem to come like a dark cloud between the soul and God, and the thought will rise— Has not God forsaken? Teach us, then, O blessed Saviour, to recall that word of loneliness upon the Cross, to remember how Thou didst know the pain, didst ask that terrible "wherefore," and "suffer us not at our last hour for any pains of death to fall from Thee."

V.—The Longing.

"I thirst."—S. John xix. 28.

The crisis of the great struggle is over. The light is beginning to return. And now the strain of effort is relaxed, the Saviour feels the parching thirst of the crucified.

Surely we are not wrong to take it quite

literally. The last word had been the cry of the human soul in separation from God; this is the cry of the human body in its weakness and longing. It was the whole of our nature which was taken into God, and Christ is not ashamed to own that He is man! And the ministry which began with hunger ends with thirst. After the conflict of the forty days He was hungered. And now upon the Cross, when the battle is over and the end is near, the Victor thirsts. Isn't it a help, just when we are getting tired with the strain of this long service, to know that Jesus Christ wasn't ashamed of the weakness of poor human nature? Because He was very God, He was not afraid to show that He was very man. How unlike that is to the false pride which, trying to make man superhuman, only succeeds in making him less than man! There is nothing of the Eastern ascetic in Christ, nothing of the Stoic in Him. He knew what was in man because He was man. He is ready to recognize and make allowance for its feebleness. He can excuse weakness as well as forgive unkindness. When the disciples could not watch with Him one hour, He does not upbraid them. He knows that "the flesh is weak." And when the multitudes came to hear Him He remembers that they "have come from far," and He will work a miracle rather than that they should "faint by the way." And it is the same on the Cross. "I am thirsty." Isn't it a help to remember that when we are very tired, and want to pray and cannot? The words won't come; or they come, but they are only words. And it seems all so miserable to be dragged down by the body. It is a real help then to think that, even when Christ was accomplishing the great atonement, He was not ashamed to say, "I am thirsty." Don't be vexed with yourselves if you can't stay all these three hours—if thoughts will wander. It seems so ungrateful to be weary before the Cross; but Christ knows how to measure love. He knew His disciples loved Him really, only they were very weak. He seems to be saying to us—

> "Well I know thy trouble,
> O my servant true!
> Thou art very weary;
> I was weary too."

Don't be ashamed to confess that bodily weakness which Christ Himself allowed.

But though I think we should be wrong not to take this word literally, it cannot be that that exhausts its meaning. The soldier in well-meant kindness offered the Crucified his sour wine. To him the cry only meant the bodily thirst which we are told the crucified felt so terribly. But to us, who have followed step by step the revelation of love, it seems as if there was some deeper meaning in the word. There is hardly one passage in the Gospels where Christ speaks of bodily hunger or thirst without in a moment passing on to the deeper needs of the soul—the thirst for the Living Water, the hunger for the Bread which came down from Heaven. Even when He sat by the well of Samaria, and asked for water from the well, He in a moment led the woman of Samaria to think of that deeper thirst which He alone could satisfy.

What is this deeper meaning of Christ's thirst upon the Cross? Surely it is the yearning of humanity for God. It is when the dark veil of separation is rent in twain, that the desolating sense of sin gives way in the sinner to the longing for God, the true Object of the soul. In Christ's word "I thirst" it seems as if human nature were crying aloud for God, no longer in bitter separation but in intense and earnest desire. When we first know God the consciousness of sin presses down upon the soul. We are separated from Him we long for. We hardly dare to look up. But when the word of pardon comes, then man feels, as he has never felt before, the claim of God. "My soul thirsteth for God, for the Living God: when shall I come to appear before the Presence of God?" "My soul thirsteth for Thee; my flesh also longeth after Thee, in a dry and thirsty land, where no water is." "I stretch forth my hands unto Thee: my soul thirsteth after Thee as a thirsty land."

Yes, the way of illumination joins on so naturally to the way of purgation. It is when the burden of sin is left before the Cross, when the brightness of God's Presence is beginning to shine upon us through the darkness, that we feel the need of more light, more knowledge of God. We want to possess Him with all the powers of our being. We do not want to know about God; we want to know Him. We long to drink of His fulness, to be flooded with His light, to live in His Presence. Our soul thirsts for "the Living God." "Oh, send forth Thy light and Thy truth. Let them lead us and bring us to Thy holy hill." When shall we be with God and "see Him as He is"? When shall we pass beyond the dark veil of

Sacraments to the unveiled Presence, and behold "the King in His Beauty"?

And because in Christ upon the Cross human nature is gathered up, that cry finds a response wherever man is man. We catch its echoes in the earnest philosophy of the ancient world, in the cry for help from heathen lands, in the deep despair of that most true, most false, of non-Christian systems, the religion of the Buddha. We hear it again, persistent or hopeless, among those in our midst who are feeling after God if haply they may find Him. In all of them man cries aloud for God; in Christ the Perfect Man that cry has found its utterance.

"I thirst." It is the thirst of humanity for God. It is our Elder Brother thirsting for that for which He came to die, the rest of man in God. It is a thirst to satisfy which He left the throne of Heaven; a thirst which two thousand years have not satisfied; a thirst which He feels now at the right hand of God; a thirst which cannot be satisfied till man attains his rest in God.

That thirst of Christ has in it, then, an element of intercession. If our thirst is His, His also is ours. If we thirst with Him, He thirsts for us. He is longing to restore each one of us to God, that we may quench our thirst at the fountain of life. Brothers and sisters, Christ is drawing us to God by the appeal of the Cross. Hasn't His love touched your heart to-day? And isn't there some poor sinful soul, lying outside the knowledge of its needs, that you may lead to God? Take him by the hand. He, too, is athirst for God. Lead him gently as you were led to the Cross of Christ.

VI.—The Triumph.

"It is finished."—S. John xix. 30.

It is the word of victory, and almost the word of death. For the last two sayings came in quick succession, and only the ear of S. John seems to have caught that word of triumph, "It is finished."

"It is finished." Two works had the Eternal Son undertaken for man—the first, to reveal the Father and declare His Name; the second, to suffer for sinners. The earlier work was finished when He had manifested the Father's Will to the world and to the chosen twelve. Hence in His High Priestly prayer He says, "I have glorified Thee upon the earth; I have finished the work which Thou gavest Me to do." But there was yet another work to do—the baptism of suffering to be baptized with, the cup of pain to be drained to the last bitter drop.

And now that, too, is finished. The love of God has been justified to the world in the Death of Christ; the Moral Law has been vindicated in His voluntary Sacrifice. And the Divine Victim looks upward with the word, "It is finished." I have done all. "Greater love hath no man than this."

"It is finished." In that one perfect and sufficient Sacrifice the sacrificial system of the ancient world found its explanation and its end. Those ancient sacrifices had dimly pointed forward, and by their very repetition had declared their impotence. It was not possible that the blood of bulls and goats could take away sins. They owed all their meaning to the fact that they were a prophecy of Calvary. There they are finished and explained. Before Good Friday they had a meaning and a function; but when Good Friday had come and gone they no longer meant anything. They were but like those survivals we see in nature, with no meaning and no purpose save as pointing back to what once they were. Christ came not to destroy, but to fulfil; not to sweep away, but to consummate. The Old Testament was no mere disciplinary code of ritual observances; it was educative and preparatory—a nurse to lead us to the school of Christ. The sin offering, which taught that without shedding of blood there is no remission, and yet that the blood of the sinner could not avail; the burnt offering, which symbolized the offering of the will to God in the sacrifice of perfect obedience; the peace offering, of which alone the offerer might partake, and which signified the reconciliation wrought by Him Who made peace by the blood of the Cross; and all the dim mysterious ritual of the great Day of Atonement, when the innocent victim, bearing the sins of the people, was led forth to the wilderness desolation;— all these were gathered up in one. "It is finished." The One Offering is made. "We have an altar," and on that altar is offered up a full, perfect, and sufficient sacrifice for the sins of the whole world.

"It is finished"—the awful conflict with the power of evil, of which we know so little. We know that power only as we feel it in ourselves, "striving, tempting, luring, goading into sin." But it cannot be but that for that awful struggle in the darkness the enemy massed his forces, and the principalities and powers of wickedness gathered round their Prince for the final conflict. And now "it is finished," the victory is won. The decisive battle has been fought, though for a little while the routed enemy may harass the followers of the Conqueror, and cut off the stragglers from the army. "Sing ye to the Lord, for He hath triumphed gloriously." He has conquered alone, but the victory is ours. Nay, "we are more than conquerors through Him that loved us."

"It is finished"—the great atonement, the work of love. No longer shall men struggle vainly, despairingly, to attain to God, building their petty Babel towers to reach to Heaven; no longer shall they offer the fruit of their body for the sin of their soul. They may dare to offer to God themselves. He has claimed the sacrifice, and accepts it as a holy offering in Christ. "It is finished." On the sixth day God finished His creative work; when, gathering up all nature into one central being, He stamped him with the image of God and rested from His finished work. But sin had marred that image which once reflected God, and now the restoration is complete, the infinite possibilities of a return to God are thrown open to man, and Christ may enter on His sabbath rest.

"It is finished"—the ancient prophecies, the old-world sacrifices, the struggle with evil, the great atonement. All is "finished." For "whom He loveth, He loveth unto the end." All through those hours of agony one power sustained the Divine Sufferer — the power of infinite love. In His image man had been created and man had fallen, and now the Eternal Son, the brightness of the Father's glory, and the express image of His Person, has been made "in the likeness of man." His is the marred visage, the weak and suffering body, the head bowed under the weight of man's transgression. Yes, He is Very Man! "made like unto His brethren," that they may be like unto Him.

"Like unto Him!" Is our love like His? When we are thinking to do some work for Him, to lead some sinful brother or sister away from the separating sin back to the rest in God, does Christ's love show itself in our love? So soon despairing, so soon cast down, so ready to say "too late," so unwilling to sacrifice self for others, so little perseverance!

Can this be love? Isn't it almost profane to apply to our half-hearted attempts at doing good a name which is the Name of God Himself? Is there any work we have ever tried to do for God, on which we can look back and say, as Christ said, "It is finished"? No! love has never "finished" till it has given all. Listen to the words of the Apostle of love: "Hereby perceive we the love of God, because He laid down His life for us: and we ought to lay down our lives for the brethren." That is the literalness of perfect love, you say; it is too high for us ordinary people. Well, dear friends, at least we may say this. We can at all events get some criterion of the likeness of our love to God's love. When the world is closing on our eyes, and our life is almost over, and eternity is very near, and the past seems all so little and so poor, if there is one bright spot on which our memory will love to linger—not in self-congratulation, God forbid!—but in great thankfulness to God, it will be some little peak in the dull level of our life which flashes back a gleam from Calvary, just some little act which meant a sacrifice of self for the love of Christ.

VII.—Rest in God.

"Father, into Thy hands I commend My spirit."—
S. Luke xxiii. 46.

It is the word of death. No, that is not true. "'Tis death itself that dies." It is the word of rest, calm, majestic, beautiful. "Father, into Thy hands!" The long and weary day is over. "It ringeth at length to evensong;" and perfect love, its work of love accomplished, bows its head upon the breast of God.

It was a word of power—the word of One Who dies by His own sovereign Will. "I lay down My life," He had said, "that I might take it again. No man taketh it from me; I lay it down of Myself. I have power to lay it down, and I have power to take it again." "Death, thou didst not come to Christ," exclaims an early Christian writer; "Christ came to thee, He Who without death could die." Yes! human nature in Christ is triumphant in death. This is not death as we know it. We have watched it in our loved ones; we have seen the enfeebled frame wrestling with all its powers, ay, and beyond its powers, with the King of Terrors, calling to its aid all those secret resources which Nature still has hidden when she seems to have done her utmost; and yet the grim lord asserts his universal reign, and man must yield. There is nothing of this in Christ. While there was aught of suffering for love to bear He waited, and now He bows His head and sleeps.

"Father!" In the unclouded brightness of God's love, the God-Man gave up the ghost. For a little while He bears that separation of the body from the soul which men call death, that in the waiting world of spirits He may be like His brethren; that loving hands may do their gentle work and prepare the Sacred Body for the tomb.

But already was that triumphant pageant beginning when the Conqueror led His captivity captive, triumphing over them gloriously; already the power of the great enemy of souls was crumbling to its fall; already to the old-world saints, the spirits in God's safe keeping, the wondrous news was proclaimed by the Redeemer Himself. "Death is conquered, man is free," the Prince of this world is crushed in the moment of his fancied triumph.

But it is not the victory, but the rest in God, on which our thoughts should dwell now and till the Easter morning. So has God loved us that by the Death of Christ He has given us the power to rest in Him. In life and in death it is the blessed right of the regenerate to rest in God, in the calm sense of restored union. All through our restless feverish life He calls us to rest in Him, not to leave our duties, but to do them in the calm consciousness that nothing shall separate us from the love of God which is in Christ Jesus our Lord. And in the Blessed Sacrament of His love, the Sacrament of union, that rest is secured. "We dwell in Christ and Christ in us; we are one with Christ and Christ with us." Who shall separate us? Our troubles, our cares, our distractions? Surely these should make us rest more perfectly in God. In the world tribulation, in Christ rest and peace—a peace which the world cannot give.

And in death? What is death? It is the gate that opens for us a more perfect life; a rest still, but a rest more holy and more calm in the Presence of our God.

"It is not exile, rest on high;
It is not sadness, peace from strife;
To fall asleep is not to die;
To dwell with Christ is better life."

Father, into Thy hands we commend our spirits in the hour of death, for Thou hast redeemed us. By the sacrifice of perfect love we are permitted even in life to rest in Thee, to know the joy of restored union, peace with God, and then perfect rest.

Brethren, you have been watching for these three hours before the Cross. You have been contemplating the revelation of love, God manifested as goodness. Is it still something external to you? or can you say, with a saint of old, " He loved me, and gave Himself for me"? Is there any region of your own personal life which has not been touched by that love, any phase of your spiritual history which has not been reflected in the Perfect Man Who for us became the Man of sorrows?

I can imagine S. Paul, the aged, as he lay in his prison at Rome awaiting the sentence of execution—I can imagine him looking back over his past life and seeing the infinite love of God reflected in it, as we have seen it before the Cross to-day. "I remember," he would say, " the time when I persecuted the Church of God and wasted it. I did it ignorantly. I knew not what I did. I knew not then, as I know now, that the Jesus Whom I persecuted was praying for me, 'Father, forgive him; he knows not what he does.' And I remember—oh, with what infinite thankfulness!—that Damascus journey, the flash of light, the pleading voice, the three days' darkness, the inward struggle, till God's grace triumphed and I prayed. And then came those wonderful words, 'Brother Saul, the Lord, even Jesus, hath sent me. Arise, and be baptized, and wash away thy sins. Why tarriest thou? To-day there is present pardon for the converted soul.' Then it comes back to me how in the joy of that pardon all my life seemed consecrated, all that was natural lifted into a higher life. I joined the little Christian Church which once I persecuted, and I seemed to hear a voice which said, ' Behold thy mother, in whom thou art reborn to God.' Yet the love of my own people, Israel according to the flesh, was not destroyed; it was lifted. I yearned that they might become in truth the Israel of God. Everything now was coloured by the Cross. I could know nothing but Jesus Christ and Him crucified. To live was Christ, to die was gain. To eat or drink, it was to the glory of God. To be made all things to all men, it was that I might save some. The Cross had transformed my life. Old things had passed away.

"And then a change comes over the scene; the brightness seems to fade out of that new life. It was only when I learned to know more of the infinite love that I realized the separating power of sin. I remember how helpless, how lonely I felt. I knew God's love. Had He not washed away my sin? and therefore I felt the hatefulness of sin. I lay at His feet as one dead. I cried aloud in my loneliness, 'I am the chief of sinners!' 'O wretched man that I am! who shall deliver me from the body of death?'

"And in a moment the clouds of darkness lifted from my soul, and hope returned, and faith grew strong; the antagonism was there still, the awful contest between the flesh and the spirit, sin and love, as real as ever, but the question, 'Who shall deliver me?' had found an answer—'I thank God through Jesus Christ our Lord.' And since then I have been learning to know more of Him and 'the power of His Resurrection,' quenching my soul-thirst from the living water. And now the end is near. 'I have fought a good fight, I have finished my course, I have kept the faith.' 'I am ready to be offered.' 'Into Thy hands, O Blessed Jesus, I commend my spirit; for Thou hast redeemed me.'"

O Love Divine, Jesus, Priest and Victim, Who on the altar of the Cross didst give Thyself for us! grant that this revelation of love may touch the heart and transform the life of those who are now alone before Thee, that, in the salvation of many, Thou mayest see of the travail of Thy soul and be satisfied, and that they whom Thou hast created for Thyself may by Thy mercy find their rest in God. Amen.

A Selection of Works

IN

THEOLOGICAL LITERATURE

PUBLISHED BY

Messrs. LONGMANS, GREEN, & CO.

39 Paternoster Row, London, E.C.

Abbey and Overton.—THE ENGLISH CHURCH IN THE EIGHTEENTH CENTURY. By Charles J. Abbey, M.A., Rector of Checkendon, Reading, and John H. Overton, M.A., Rector of Epworth; Rural Dean of Isle of Axholme. *Crown 8vo. 7s. 6d.*

Adams.—SACRED ALLEGORIES. The Shadow of the Cross—The Distant Hills—The Old Man's Home—The King's Messengers. By the Rev. William Adams, M.A. *Crown 8vo. 3s. 6d.*
    The four Allegories may be had separately, with Illustrations. *16mo. 1s. each.*

Aids to the Inner Life.
    Edited by the Rev. W. H. Hutchings, M.A., Rector of Kirkby Misperton, Yorkshire. *Five Vols. 32mo, cloth limp, 6d. each; or cloth extra, 1s. each.*
    With red borders, 2s. each. Sold separately.
    OF THE IMITATION OF CHRIST. By Thomas à Kempis.
    THE CHRISTIAN YEAR.
    THE DEVOUT LIFE. By St. Francis de Sales.
    THE HIDDEN LIFE OF THE SOUL.
    THE SPIRITUAL COMBAT. By Laurence Scupoli.

Allen.—THE CHURCH CATECHISM: its History and Contents. A Manual for Teachers and Students. By the Rev. A. J. C. Allen, M.A., formerly Principal of the Chester Diocesan Training College. *Crown 8vo. 3s. 6d.*

Barnes.—CANONICAL AND UNCANONICAL GOSPELS. With a Translation of the recently discovered Fragment of the 'Gospel of St. Peter,' and a Selection from the Sayings of our Lord not recorded in the Four Gospels. By W. E. Barnes, B.D., Theological Lecturer at Clare College, Cambridge. *Crown 8vo. 3s. 6d.*

Barry.—SOME LIGHTS OF SCIENCE ON THE FAITH. Being the Bampton Lectures for 1892. By the Right Rev. Alfred Barry, D.D., Canon of Windsor, formerly Bishop of Sydney, Metropolitan of New South Wales, and Primate of Australia. *8vo. 12s. 6d.*

Bathe.—Works by the Rev. ANTHONY BATHE, M.A.
    A LENT WITH JESUS. A Plain Guide for Churchmen. Containing Readings for Lent and Easter Week, and on the Holy Eucharist. 32mo, 1s.; *or in paper cover*, 6d.
    AN ADVENT WITH JESUS. 32mo, 1s.; *or in paper cover*, 6d.
    WHAT I SHOULD BELIEVE. A Simple Manual of Self-Instruction for Church People. *Crown 8vo.* 3s. 6d.

Benson.—THE FINAL PASSOVER: A Series of Meditations upon the Passion of our Lord Jesus Christ. By the Rev. R. M. BENSON, M.A., Student of Christ Church, Oxford. *Small 8vo.*
    Vol. I.—THE REJECTION. 5s. | Vol. III.—THE DIVINE EXODUS.
    Vol. II.—THE UPPER CHAMBER. | Parts I. and II. 5s. each.
        [*In preparation.*
    Vol. IV.—THE LIFE BEYOND THE GRAVE. 5s.

Bickersteth.—YESTERDAY, TO-DAY, AND FOR EVER: a Poem in Twelve Books. By EDWARD HENRY BICKERSTETH, D.D., Bishop of Exeter. *One Shilling Edition*, 18mo. *With red borders*, 16mo, 2s. 6d.
    The Crown 8vo Edition (5s.) *may still be had.*

Blunt.—Works by the Rev. JOHN HENRY BLUNT, D.D.
    THE ANNOTATED BOOK OF COMMON PRAYER: Being an Historical, Ritual, and Theological Commentary on the Devotional System of the Church of England. *4to.* 21s.
    THE COMPENDIOUS EDITION OF THE ANNOTATED BOOK OF COMMON PRAYER: Forming a concise Commentary on the Devotional System of the Church of England. *Crown 8vo.* 10s. 6d.
    DICTIONARY OF DOCTRINAL AND HISTORICAL THEOLOGY. By various Writers. *Imperial 8vo.* 21s.
    DICTIONARY OF SECTS, HERESIES, ECCLESIASTICAL PARTIES AND SCHOOLS OF RELIGIOUS THOUGHT. By various Writers. *Imperial 8vo.* 21s.
    THE BOOK OF CHURCH LAW. Being an Exposition of the Legal Rights and Duties of the Parochial Clergy and the Laity of the Church of England. Revised by Sir WALTER G. F. PHILLIMORE, Bart., D.C.L. *Crown 8vo.* 7s. 6d.
    A COMPANION TO THE BIBLE: Being a Plain Commentary on Scripture History, to the end of the Apostolic Age. *Two Vols. small 8vo. Sold separately.*
    THE OLD TESTAMENT. 3s. 6d.   THE NEW TESTAMENT. 3s. 6d.
    HOUSEHOLD THEOLOGY: a Handbook of Religious Information respecting the Holy Bible, the Prayer Book, the Church, etc., etc. *Paper cover*, 16mo. 1s. *Also the Larger Edition*, 3s. 6d.

Body.—Works by the Rev. GEORGE BODY, D.D., Canon of Durham.
    THE LIFE OF LOVE. A Course of Lent Lectures. *Crown 8vo.* 4s. 6d.
    THE SCHOOL OF CALVARY; or, Laws of Christian Life revealed from the Cross. 16mo. 2s. 6d.
    THE LIFE OF JUSTIFICATION. 16mo. 2s. 6d.
    THE LIFE OF TEMPTATION. 16mo. 2s. 6d.

IN THEOLOGICAL LITERATURE. 3

Bonney.—CHRISTIAN DOCTRINES AND MODERN THOUGHT: being the Boyle Lectures for 1891. By the Rev. T. G. BONNEY, D.Sc., Hon. Canon of Manchester. *Crown 8vo.* 5s.

Boultbee.—A COMMENTARY ON THE THIRTY-NINE ARTICLES OF THE CHURCH OF ENGLAND. By the Rev. T. P. BOULTBEE, formerly Principal of the London College of Divinity, St. John's Hall, Highbury. *Crown 8vo.* 6s.

Bright.—Works by WILLIAM BRIGHT, D.D., Canon of Christ Church, Oxford.
WAYMARKS IN CHURCH HISTORY. *Crown 8vo.*
MORALITY IN DOCTRINE. *Crown 8vo.* 7s. 6d.
LESSONS FROM THE LIVES OF THREE GREAT FATHERS: St. Athanasius, St. Chrysostom, and St. Augustine. *Crown 8vo.* 6s.
THE INCARNATION AS A MOTIVE POWER. *Crown 8vo.* 6s.

Bright and Medd.—LIBER PRECUM PUBLICARUM ECCLESIÆ ANGLICANÆ. A GULIELMO BRIGHT, S.T.P., et PETRO GOLDSMITH MEDD, A.M., Latine redditus. *Small 8vo.* 7s. 6d.

Browne.—AN EXPOSITION OF THE THIRTY-NINE ARTICLES, Historical and Doctrinal. By E. H. BROWNE, D.D., formerly Bishop of Winchester. *8vo.* 16s.

Campion and Beamont.—THE PRAYER BOOK INTERLEAVED. With Historical Illustrations and Explanatory Notes arranged parallel to the Text. By W. M. CAMPION, D.D., and W. J. BEAMONT, M.A. *Small 8vo.* 7s. 6d.

Carter.—Works edited by the Rev. T. T. CARTER, M.A., Hon. Canon of Christ Church, Oxford.
THE TREASURY OF DEVOTION: a Manual of Prayer for General and Daily Use. Compiled by a Priest. *18mo.* 2s. 6d.; *cloth limp*, 2s.; or bound with the Book of Common Prayer, 3s. 6d. *Large-Type Edition. Crown 8vo.* 3s. 6d.
THE WAY OF LIFE: A Book of Prayers and Instruction for the Young at School, with a Preparation for Confirmation. Compiled by a Priest, *18mo.* 1s. 6d.
THE PATH OF HOLINESS: a First Book of Prayers, with the Service of the Holy Communion, for the Young. Compiled by a Priest. With Illustrations. *16mo.* 1s. 6d.; *cloth limp*, 1s.
THE GUIDE TO HEAVEN: a Book of Prayers for every Want. (For the Working Classes.) Compiled by a Priest. *18mo.* 1s. 6d.; *cloth limp*, 1s. *Large-Type Edition. Crown 8vo.* 1s. 6d.; *cloth limp*, 1s.

[continued.

Carter.—Works edited by the Rev. T. T. CARTER, M.A., Hon. Canon of Christ Church, Oxford—*continued.*
   SELF-RENUNCIATION. 16mo. 2s. 6d.
   THE STAR OF CHILDHOOD: a First Book of Prayers and Instruction for Children. Compiled by a Priest. With Illustrations. 16mo. 2s. 6d.
   NICHOLAS FERRAR: his Household and his Friends. With Portrait engraved after a Picture by CORNELIUS JANSSEN at Magdalene College, Cambridge. *Crown 8vo. 6s.*

Carter.—MAXIMS AND GLEANINGS FROM THE WRITINGS OF T. T. CARTER, M.A. Selected and arranged for Daily Use. *Crown 16mo. 1s.*

Conybeare and Howson.—THE LIFE AND EPISTLES OF ST. PAUL. By the Rev. W. J. CONYBEARE, M.A., and the Very Rev. J. S. HOWSON, D.D. With numerous Maps and Illustrations.
   LIBRARY EDITION. *Two Vols. 8vo. 21s.*
   STUDENTS' EDITION. *One Vol. Crown 8vo. 6s.*
   POPULAR EDITION. *One Vol. Crown 8vo. 3s. 6d.*

Copleston.—BUDDHISM—PRIMITIVE AND PRESENT IN MAGADHA AND IN CEYLON. By REGINALD STEPHEN COPLESTON, D.D., Bishop of Colombo. *8vo. 16s.*

Devotional Series, 16mo, Red Borders. *Each 2s. 6d.*
   BICKERSTETH'S YESTERDAY, TO-DAY, AND FOR EVER.
   CHILCOT'S TREATISE ON EVIL THOUGHTS.
   THE CHRISTIAN YEAR.
   FRANCIS DE SALES' (ST.) THE DEVOUT LIFE.
   HERBERT'S POEMS AND PROVERBS.
   KEMPIS' (À) OF THE IMITATION OF CHRIST.
   WILSON'S THE LORD'S SUPPER. *Large type.*
   *TAYLOR'S (JEREMY) HOLY LIVING.
   *——— ——— HOLY DYING.
        * *These two in one Volume. 5s.*

Devotional Series, 18mo, without Red Borders. *Each 1s.*
   BICKERSTETH'S YESTERDAY, TO-DAY, AND FOR EVER.
   THE CHRISTIAN YEAR.
   FRANCIS DE SALES' (ST.) THE DEVOUT LIFE.
   HERBERT'S POEMS AND PROVERBS.
   KEMPIS (À) OF THE IMITATION OF CHRIST.
   WILSON'S THE LORD'S SUPPER, *Large type.*
   *TAYLOR'S (JEREMY) HOLY LIVING.
   *——— ——— HOLY DYING.
        * *These two in one Volume. 2s. 6d.*

Edersheim.—Works by ALFRED EDERSHEIM, M.A., D.D., Ph.D., sometime Grinfield Lecturer on the Septuagint, Oxford.

THE LIFE AND TIMES OF JESUS THE MESSIAH. *Two Vols.* 8*vo.* 24*s.*

JESUS THE MESSIAH : being an Abridged Edition of 'The Life and Times of Jesus the Messiah.' *Crown* 8*vo.* 7*s.* 6*d.*

PROPHECY AND HISTORY IN RELATION TO THE MESSIAH : The Warburton Lectures, 1880-1884. 8*vo.* 12*s.*

Ellicott.—Works by C. J. ELLICOTT, D.D., Bishop of Gloucester and Bristol.

A CRITICAL AND GRAMMATICAL COMMENTARY ON ST. PAUL'S EPISTLES. Greek Text, with a Critical and Grammatical Commentary, and a Revised English Translation. 8*vo.*

1 CORINTHIANS. 16*s.*	PHILIPPIANS, COLOSSIANS, AND PHILEMON. 10*s.* 6*d.*
GALATIANS. 8*s.* 6*d.*	
EPHESIANS. 8*s.* 6*d.*	THESSALONIANS. 7*s.* 6*d.*

PASTORAL EPISTLES. 10*s.* 6*d.*

HISTORICAL LECTURES ON THE LIFE OF OUR LORD JESUS CHRIST. 8*vo.* 12*s.*

Epochs of Church History.—Edited by MANDELL CREIGHTON, D.D., LL.D., Bishop of Peterborough. *Fcap.* 8*vo.* 2*s.* 6*d.* each.

THE ENGLISH CHURCH IN OTHER LANDS. By the Rev. H. W. TUCKER, M.A.

THE HISTORY OF THE REFORMATION IN ENGLAND. By the Rev. GEO. G. PERRY, M.A.

THE CHURCH OF THE EARLY FATHERS. By the Rev. ALFRED PLUMMER, D.D.

THE EVANGELICAL REVIVAL IN THE EIGHTEENTH CENTURY. By the Rev. J. H. OVERTON, M.A.

THE UNIVERSITY OF OXFORD. By the Hon. G. C. BRODRICK, D.C.L.

THE UNIVERSITY OF CAMBRIDGE. By J. BASS MULLINGER, M.A.

THE ENGLISH CHURCH IN THE MIDDLE AGES. By the Rev. W. HUNT, M.A.

THE CHURCH AND THE EASTERN EMPIRE. By the Rev. H. F. TOZER, M.A.

THE CHURCH AND THE ROMAN EMPIRE. By the Rev. A. CARR.

THE CHURCH AND THE PURITANS, 1570-1660. By HENRY OFFLEY WAKEMAN, M.A.

HILDEBRAND AND HIS TIMES. By the Rev. W. R. W. STEPHENS, M.A.

THE POPES AND THE HOHENSTAUFEN. By UGO BALZANI.

THE COUNTER REFORMATION. By ADOLPHUS WILLIAM WARD, Litt.D.

WYCLIFFE AND MOVEMENTS FOR REFORM. By REGINALD L. POOLE, M.A.

THE ARIAN CONTROVERSY. By H. M. GWATKIN, M.A.

Fosbery.—Works edited by the Rev. THOMAS VINCENT FOSBERY, M.A., sometime Vicar of St. Giles's, Reading.

VOICES OF COMFORT. *Cheap Edition. Small 8vo.* 3s. 6d.
The Larger Edition (7s. 6d.) may still be had.

HYMNS AND POEMS FOR THE SICK AND SUFFERING. In connection with the Service for the Visitation of the Sick. Selected from Various Authors. *Small 8vo.* 3s. 6d.

Gore.—Works by the Rev. CHARLES GORE, M.A., Principal of the Pusey House; Fellow of Trinity College, Oxford.

THE MINISTRY OF THE CHRISTIAN CHURCH. 8vo. 10s. 6d.
ROMAN CATHOLIC CLAIMS. *Crown 8vo.* 3s. 6d.

Goulburn.—Works by EDWARD MEYRICK GOULBURN, D.D., D.C.L., sometime Dean of Norwich.

THOUGHTS ON PERSONAL RELIGION. *Small 8vo.* 6s. 6d. *Cheap Edition,* 3s. 6d. ; *Presentation Edition,* 2 vols. small 8vo, 10s. 6d.

THE PURSUIT OF HOLINESS: a Sequel to 'Thoughts on Personal Religion.' *Small 8vo.* 5s. *Cheap Edition.* 3s. 6d.

THE GOSPEL OF THE CHILDHOOD: a Practical and Devotional Commentary on the Single Incident of our Blessed Lord's Childhood (St. Luke ii. 41 to the end). *Crown 8vo.* 2s. 6d.

THE COLLECTS OF THE DAY: an Exposition, Critical and Devotional, of the Collects appointed at the Communion. With Preliminary Essays on their Structure, Sources, etc. 2 vols. *Crown 8vo.* 8s. each.

THOUGHTS UPON THE LITURGICAL GOSPELS for the Sundays, one for each day in the year. With an Introduction on their Origin, History, the modifications made in them by the Reformers and by the Revisers of the Prayer Book. 2 vols. *Crown 8vo.* 16s.

MEDITATIONS UPON THE LITURGICAL GOSPELS for the Minor Festivals of Christ, the two first Week-days of the Easter and Whitsun Festivals, and the Red-letter Saints' Days. *Crown 8vo.* 8s. 6d.

FAMILY PRAYERS, compiled from various sources (chiefly from Bishop Hamilton's Manual), and arranged on the Liturgical Principle. *Crown 8vo.* 3s. 6d. *Cheap Edition.* 16mo. 1s.

Harrison.—Works by the Rev. ALEXANDER J. HARRISON, B.D., Lecturer of the Christian Evidence Society.

PROBLEMS OF CHRISTIANITY AND SCEPTICISM ; Lessons from Twenty Years' Experience in the Field of Christian Evidence. *Crown 8vo.* 7s. 6d.

THE CHURCH IN RELATION TO SCEPTICS : a Conversational Guide to Evidential Work. *Crown 8vo.* 7s. 6d.

Holland.—Works by the Rev. HENRY SCOTT HOLLAND, M.A., Canon and Precentor of St. Paul's.

> THE CITY OF GOD AND THE COMING OF THE KINGDOM: Four Addresses delivered at St. Asaph on the Spiritual and Ethical Value of Belief in the Church. To which are added Sermons on kindred subjects. *Crown 8vo. 7s. 6d.*
>
> PLEAS AND CLAIMS FOR CHRIST. *Crown 8vo. 7s. 6d.*
>
> CREED AND CHARACTER: Sermons. *Crown 8vo. 3s. 6d.*
>
> ON BEHALF OF BELIEF. Sermons preached in St. Paul's Cathedral. *Crown 8vo. 3s. 6d.*
>
> CHRIST OR ECCLESIASTES. Sermons preached in St. Paul's Cathedral. *Crown 8vo. 2s. 6d.*
>
> LOGIC AND LIFE, with other Sermons. *Crown 8vo. 3s. 6d.*

Hopkins.—CHRIST THE CONSOLER. A Book of Comfort for the Sick. By ELLICE HOPKINS. *Small 8vo. 2s. 6d.*

Ingram.—HAPPINESS IN THE SPIRITUAL LIFE; or, 'The Secret of the Lord.' A Series of Practical Considerations. By W. CLAVELL INGRAM, D.D., Dean of Peterborough. *Crown 8vo. 7s. 6d.*

INHERITANCE OF THE SAINTS; or, Thoughts on the Communion of Saints and the Life of the World to come. Collected chiefly from English Writers by L. P. With a Preface by the Rev. HENRY SCOTT HOLLAND, M.A. *Crown 8vo. 7s. 6d.*

Jameson.—Works by Mrs. JAMESON.

> SACRED AND LEGENDARY ART, containing Legends of the Angels and Archangels, the Evangelists, the Apostles. With 19 Etchings and 187 Woodcuts. *Two vols. Cloth, gilt top, 20s. net.*
>
> LEGENDS OF THE MONASTIC ORDERS, as represented in the Fine Arts. With 11 Etchings and 88 Woodcuts. *One Vol. Cloth, gilt top, 10s. net.*
>
> LEGENDS OF THE MADONNA, OR BLESSED VIRGIN MARY. With 27 Etchings and 165 Woodcuts. *One Vol. Cloth, gilt top, 10s. net.*
>
> THE HISTORY OF OUR LORD, as exemplified in Works of Art. Commenced by the late Mrs. JAMESON; continued and completed by LADY EASTLAKE. With 31 Etchings and 281 Woodcuts. *Two Vols. 8vo. 20s. net.*

Jennings.—ECCLESIA ANGLICANA. A History of the Church of Christ in England from the Earliest to the Present Times. By the Rev. ARTHUR CHARLES JENNINGS, M.A. *Crown 8vo. 7s. 6d.*

Jukes.—Works by ANDREW JUKES.
>   THE NEW MAN AND THE ETERNAL LIFE. Notes on the Reiterated Amens of the Son of God. *Crown 8vo.* 6s.
>   THE NAMES OF GOD IN HOLY SCRIPTURE: a Revelation of His Nature and Relationships. *Crown 8vo.* 4s. 6d.
>   THE TYPES OF GENESIS. *Crown 8vo.* 7s. 6d.
>   THE SECOND DEATH AND THE RESTITUTION OF ALL THINGS. *Crown 8vo.* 3s. 6d.
>   THE MYSTERY OF THE KINGDOM. *Crown 8vo.* 2s. 6d.
>   THE ORDER AND CONNEXION OF THE CHURCH'S TEACHING, as set forth in the arrangement of the Epistles and Gospels throughout the Year. *Crown 8vo.* 2s. 6d.

King.—DR. LIDDON'S TOUR IN EGYPT AND PALESTINE IN 1886. Being Letters descriptive of the Tour, written by his Sister, Mrs. KING. *Crown 8vo.* 5s.

Knox Little.—Works by W. J. KNOX LITTLE, M.A., Canon Residentiary of Worcester, and Vicar of Hoar Cross.
>   SACERDOTALISM, WHEN RIGHTLY UNDERSTOOD, THE TEACHING OF THE CHURCH OF ENGLAND: being a Letter addressed in Four Parts to the Very Rev. WILLIAM J. BUTLER, D.D., Dean of Lincoln, etc., etc. *Crown 8vo.* 6s.; *or in Four Parts, price* 1s. *each net.*
>> Part I. CONFESSION AND ABSOLUTION.
>> Part II. FASTING COMMUNION AND EUCHARISTIC WORSHIP.
>> Part III. THE REAL PRESENCE AND THE EUCHARISTIC SACRIFICE.
>> Part IV. THE APOSTOLIC MINISTRY.
>   SKETCHES IN SUNSHINE AND STORM: a Collection of Miscellaneous Essays and Notes of Travel. *Crown 8vo.* 7s. 6d.
>   THE CHRISTIAN HOME. *Crown 8vo.* 6s. 6d.
>   THE HOPES AND DECISIONS OF THE PASSION OF OUR MOST HOLY REDEEMER. *Crown 8vo.* 2s. 6d.
>   CHARACTERISTICS AND MOTIVES OF THE CHRISTIAN LIFE. Ten Sermons preached in Manchester Cathedral, in Lent and Advent. *Crown 8vo.* 2s. 6d.
>   SERMONS PREACHED FOR THE MOST PART IN MANCHESTER. *Crown 8vo.* 3s. 6d.
>   THE MYSTERY OF THE PASSION OF OUR MOST HOLY REDEEMER. *Crown 8vo.* 2s. 6d.

[*continued.*

IN THEOLOGICAL LITERATURE. 9

Knox Little.—Works by W. J. KNOX LITTLE, M.A., Canon Residentiary of Worcester, and Vicar of Hoar Cross.—*continued.*

THE WITNESS OF THE PASSION OF OUR MOST HOLY REDEEMER. *Crown 8vo.* 2s. 6d.

THE LIGHT OF LIFE. Sermons preached on Various Occasions. *Crown 8vo.* 3s. 6d.

SUNLIGHT AND SHADOW IN THE CHRISTIAN LIFE. Sermons preached for the most part in America. *Crown 8vo.* 3s. 6d.

Lear.—Works by, and Edited by, H. L. SIDNEY LEAR.

FOR DAYS AND YEARS. A book containing a Text, Short Reading, and Hymn for Every Day in the Church's Year. 16mo. 2s. 6d. *Also a Cheap Edition,* 32mo. 1s.; *or cloth gilt,* 1s. 6d.

FIVE MINUTES. Daily Readings of Poetry. 16mo. 3s. 6d. *Also a Cheap Edition,* 32mo. 1s.; *or cloth gilt,* 1s. 6d.

WEARINESS. A Book for the Languid and Lonely. *Large Type. Small 8vo.* 5s.

THE LIGHT OF THE CONSCIENCE. 16mo. 2s. 6d. 32mo. 1s.; *cloth limp,* 6d.

CHRISTIAN BIOGRAPHIES. *Nine Vols. Crown 8vo.* 3s. 6d. *each.*

MADAME LOUISE DE FRANCE, Daughter of Louis XV., known also as the Mother Térèse de St. Augustin.

A DOMINICAN ARTIST: a Sketch of the Life of the Rev. Père Besson, of the Order of St. Dominic.

HENRI PERREYVE. By A. GRATRY.

ST. FRANCIS DE SALES, Bishop and Prince of Geneva.

THE REVIVAL OF PRIESTLY LIFE IN THE SEVENTEENTH CENTURY IN FRANCE.

A CHRISTIAN PAINTER OF THE NINETEENTH CENTURY.

BOSSUET AND HIS CONTEMPORARIES.

FÉNELON, ARCHBISHOP OF CAMBRAI.

HENRI DOMINIQUE LACORDAIRE.

DEVOTIONAL WORKS. Edited by H. L. SIDNEY LEAR. *New and Uniform Editions. Nine Vols.* 16mo. 2s. 6d. *each.*

FÉNELON'S SPIRITUAL LETTERS TO MEN.

FÉNELON'S SPIRITUAL LETTERS TO WOMEN.

A SELECTION FROM THE SPIRITUAL LETTERS OF ST. FRANCIS DE SALES.

THE SPIRIT OF ST. FRANCIS DE SALES.

THE HIDDEN LIFE OF THE SOUL.

THE LIGHT OF THE CONSCIENCE.

SELF-RENUNCIATION. From the French.

ST. FRANCIS DE SALES' OF THE LOVE OF GOD.

SELECTIONS FROM PASCAL'S 'THOUGHTS.'

Liddon.—Works by HENRY PARRY LIDDON, D.D., D.C.L., LL.D., late Canon Residentiary and Chancellor of St. Paul's.

LIFE OF EDWARD BOUVERIE PUSEY, D.D. By HENRY PARRY LIDDON, D.D., D.C.L., LL.D. Edited and prepared for publication by the Rev. J. O. JOHNSTON, M A., Vicar of All Saints', Oxford; and the Rev. ROBERT J. WILSON, M.A., Warden of Keble College. *Four Vols.* 8*vo.* *Vols. I. and II., with 2 Portraits and 7 Illustrations.* 36*s.*

ESSAYS AND ADDRESSES: Lectures on Buddhism—Lectures on the Life of St. Paul—Papers on Dante. *Crown* 8*vo.* 5*s.*

EXPLANATORY ANALYSIS OF PAUL'S EPISTLE TO THE ROMANS. 8*vo.* 14*s.*

SERMONS ON OLD TESTAMENT SUBJECTS. *Crown* 8*vo.* 5*s.*

SERMONS ON SOME WORDS OF CHRIST. *Crown* 8*vo.* 5*s.*

THE DIVINITY OF OUR LORD AND SAVIOUR JESUS CHRIST. Being the Bampton Lectures for 1866. *Crown* 8*vo.* 5*s.*

ADVENT IN ST. PAUL'S. Sermons bearing chiefly on the Two Comings of our Lord. *Two Vols. Crown* 8*vo.* 3*s.* 6*d. each. Cheap Edition in one Volume. Crown* 8*vo.* 5*s.*

CHRISTMASTIDE IN ST. PAUL'S. Sermons bearing chiefly on the Birth of our Lord and the End of the Year. *Crown* 8*vo.* 5*s.*

PASSIONTIDE SERMONS. *Crown* 8*vo.* 5*s.*

EASTER IN ST. PAUL'S. Sermons bearing chiefly on the Resurrection of our Lord. *Two Vols. Crown* 8*vo.* 3*s.* 6*d. each. Cheap Edition in one Volume. Crown* 8*vo.* 5*s.*

SERMONS PREACHED BEFORE THE UNIVERSITY OF OXFORD. *Two Vols. Crown* 8*vo.* 3*s.* 6*d. each. Cheap Edition in one Volume. Crown* 8*vo.* 5*s.*

THE MAGNIFICAT. Sermons in St. Paul's. *Crown* 8*vo.* 2*s.* 6*d.*

SOME ELEMENTS OF RELIGION. Lent Lectures. *Small* 8*vo.* 2*s.* 6*d.*; *or in paper cover,* 1*s.* 6*d.*
 The Crown 8*vo Edition* (5*s.*) *may still be had.*

SELECTIONS FROM THE WRITINGS OF H. P. LIDDON, D.D. *Crown* 8*vo.* 3*s.* 6*d.*

MAXIMS AND GLEANINGS FROM THE WRITINGS OF H. P. LIDDON, D.D. Selected and arranged by C. M. S. *Crown* 16*mo.* 1*s.*

DR. LIDDON'S TOUR IN EGYPT AND PALESTINE IN 1886. Being Letters descriptive of the Tour, written by his Sister, Mrs. KING. *Crown* 8*vo.* 5*s.*

Luckock.—Works by HERBERT MORTIMER LUCKOCK, D.D., Dean of Lichfield.

AFTER DEATH. An Examination of the Testimony of Primitive Times respecting the State of the Faithful Dead, and their Relationship to the Living. *Crown 8vo. 6s.*

THE INTERMEDIATE STATE BETWEEN DEATH AND JUDGMENT. Being a Sequel to *After death*. *Crown 8vo. 6s.*

FOOTPRINTS OF THE SON OF MAN, as traced by St. Mark. Being Eighty Portions for Private Study, Family Reading, and Instructions in Church. *Two Vols. Crown 8vo. 12s.* Cheap Edition in one Vol. *Crown 8vo. 5s.*

THE DIVINE LITURGY. Being the Order for Holy Communion, Historically, Doctrinally, and devotionally set forth, in Fifty Portions. *Crown 8vo. 6s.*

STUDIES IN THE HISTORY OF THE BOOK OF COMMON PRAYER. The Anglican Reform—The Puritan Innovations—The Elizabethan Reaction—The Caroline Settlement. With Appendices. *Crown 8vo. 6s.*

THE BISHOPS IN THE TOWER. A Record of Stirring Events affecting the Church and Nonconformists from the Restoration to the Revolution. *Crown 8vo. 6s.*

LYRA GERMANICA. Hymns translated from the German by CATHERINE WINKWORTH. *Small 8vo. 5s.*

MacColl.—CHRISTIANITY IN RELATION TO SCIENCE AND MORALS. By the Rev. MALCOLM MACCOLL, M.A., Canon Residentiary of Ripon. *Crown 8vo. 6s.*

Mason.—Works by A. J. MASON, D.D., Hon. Canon of Canterbury and Examining Chaplain to the Archbishop of Canterbury.

THE FAITH OF THE GOSPEL. A Manual of Christian Doctrine. *Crown 8vo. 3s. 6d.*

THE RELATION OF CONFIRMATION TO BAPTISM. As taught in Holy Scripture and the Fathers. *Crown 8vo. 7s. 6d.*

Mercier.—OUR MOTHER CHURCH : Being Simple Talk on High Topics. By Mrs. JEROME MERCIER. *Small 8vo.* 3s. 6d.

Molesworth.—STORIES OF THE SAINTS FOR CHILDREN : The Black Letter Saints. By Mrs. MOLESWORTH, Author of 'The Palace in the Garden,' etc, etc. *With Illustrations. Royal 16mo.* 5s.

Mozley.—Works by J. B. MOZLEY, D.D., late Canon of Christ Church, and Regius Professor of Divinity at Oxford.

ESSAYS, HISTORICAL AND THEOLOGICAL. *Two Vols. 8vo.* 24s.

EIGHT LECTURES ON MIRACLES. Being the Bampton Lectures for 1865. *Crown 8vo.* 7s. 6d.

RULING IDEAS IN EARLY AGES AND THEIR RELATION TO OLD TESTAMENT FAITH. Lectures delivered to Graduates of the University of Oxford. *8vo.* 10s. 6d.

SERMONS PREACHED BEFORE THE UNIVERSITY OF OXFORD, and on Various Occasions. *Crown 8vo.* 7s. 6d.

SERMONS, PAROCHIAL AND OCCASIONAL. *Crown 8vo.* 7s. 6d.

Newbolt.—Works by the Rev. W. C. E. NEWBOLT, M.A., Canon and Chancellor of St. Paul's Cathedral, Select Preacher at Oxford, and Examining Chaplain to the Lord Bishop of Ely.

SPECULUM SACERDOTUM ; or, the Divine Model of the Priestly Life. *Crown 8vo.* 7s. 6d.

THE FRUIT OF THE SPIRIT. Being Ten Addresses bearing on the Spiritual Life. *Crown 8vo.* 2s. 6d.

THE MAN OF GOD. Being Six Addresses delivered during Lent at the Primary Ordination of the Right Rev. the Lord Alwyne Compton, D.D., Bishop of Ely. *Small 8vo.* 1s. 6d.

THE PRAYER BOOK : Its Voice and Teaching. Being Spiritual Addresses bearing on the Book of Common Prayer. *Crown 8vo.* 2s. 6d.

Newnham.—THE ALL-FATHER : Sermons preached in a Village Church. By the Rev. H. P. NEWNHAM. With Preface by EDNA LYALL. *Crown 8vo.* 4s. 6d.

IN THEOLOGICAL LITERATURE. 13

Newman.—Works by JOHN HENRY NEWMAN, B.D., sometime Vicar of St. Mary's, Oxford.

PAROCHIAL AND PLAIN SERMONS. *Eight Vols. Cabinet Edition. Crown 8vo.* 5s. *each. Cheaper Edition.* 3s. 6d. *each.*

SELECTION, ADAPTED TO THE SEASONS OF THE ECCLESIASTICAL YEAR, from the 'Parochial and Plain Sermons,' *Cabinet Edition. Crown 8vo.* 5s. *Cheaper Edition.* 3s. 6d.

FIFTEEN SERMONS PREACHED BEFORE THE UNIVERSITY OF OXFORD *Cabinet Edition. Crown 8vo.* 5s. *Cheaper Edition.* 3s. 6d.

SERMONS BEARING UPON SUBJECTS OF THE DAY. *Cabinet Edition. Crown 8vo.* 5s. *Cheaper Edition. Crown 8vo.* 3s. 6d.

LECTURES ON THE DOCTRINE OF JUSTIFICATION. *Cabinet Edition Crown 8vo.* 5s. *Cheaper Edition.* 3s. 6d.

** *A Complete List of Cardinal Newman's Works can be had on Application.*

Osborne.—Works by EDWARD OSBORNE, Mission Priest of the Society of St. John the Evangelist, Cowley, Oxford.

THE CHILDREN'S SAVIOUR. Instructions to Children on the Life of Our Lord and Saviour Jesus Christ. *Illustrated.* 16mo. 2s. 6d.

THE SAVIOUR KING. Instructions to Children on Old Testament Types and Illustrations of the Life of Christ. *Illustrated.* 16mo. 2s. 6d.

THE CHILDREN'S FAITH. Instructions to Children on the Apostles' Creed. *Illustrated.* 16mo. 2s. 6d.

Overton.—THE ENGLISH CHURCH IN THE NINETEENTH CENTURY. By the Rev. JOHN H. OVERTON, M.A., Canon of Lincoln, Rector of Epworth, Doncaster, and Rural Dean of the Isle of Axholme. 8vo. 14s.

Oxenden.—Works by the Right Rev. ASHTON OXENDEN, formerly Bishop of Montreal.

PLAIN SERMONS, to which is prefixed a Memorial Portrait. *Crown 8vo.* 5s.

THE HISTORY OF MY LIFE: An Autobiography. *Crown 8vo.* 5s.

PEACE AND ITS HINDRANCES. *Crown 8vo.* 1s. *sewed*, 2s. *cloth.*

THE PATHWAY OF SAFETY; or, Counsel to the Awakened. *Fcap. 8vo, large type.* 2s. 6d. *Cheap Edition. Small type, limp,* 1s.

THE EARNEST COMMUNICANT. *New Red Rubric Edition.* 32mo, *cloth.* 2s. *Common Edition.* 32mo. 1s.

OUR CHURCH AND HER SERVICES. *Fcap. 8vo.* 2s. 6d.

[continued.

Oxenden.—Works by the Right Rev. ASHTON OXENDEN formerly Bishop of Montreal—*continued.*
   FAMILY PRAYERS FOR FOUR WEEKS. First Series. *Fcap. 8vo.* 2s. 6d. Second Series. *Fcap. 8vo.* 2s. 6d.
      LARGE TYPE EDITION. Two Series in one Volume. *Crown 8vo.* 6s.
   COTTAGE SERMONS; or, Plain Words to the Poor. *Fcap. 8vo.* 2s. 6d.
   THOUGHTS FOR HOLY WEEK. *16mo, cloth.* 1s. 6d.
   DECISION. *18mo.* 1s. 6d.
   THE HOME BEYOND; or, A Happy Old Age. *Fcap. 8vo.* 1s. 6d.
   THE LABOURING MAN'S BOOK. *18mo, large type, cloth.* 1s. 6d.

Paget.—Works by FRANCIS PAGET, D.D., Dean of Christ Church, Oxford.
   THE SPIRIT OF DISCIPLINE: Sermons. *Crown 8vo.* 6s. 6d.
   FACULTIES AND DIFFICULTIES FOR BELIEF AND DISBELIEF. *Crown 8vo.* 6s. 6d.
   THE HALLOWING OF WORK. Addresses given at Eton, January, 16-18, 1888. *Small 8vo.* 2s.

PRACTICAL REFLECTIONS. By a CLERGYMAN. With Prefaces by H. P. LIDDON, D.D., D.C.L., and the BISHOP OF LINCOLN. *Crown 8vo.*
   THE HOLY GOSPELS. 4s. 6d. | THE PSALMS. 5s.
   ACTS TO REVELATIONS. 6s. | THE BOOK OF GENESIS. 4s. 6d.

PRIEST (THE) TO THE ALTAR; or, Aids to the Devout Celebration of Holy Communion, chiefly after the Ancient English Use of Sarum. *Royal 8vo.* 12s.

Puller.—THE PRIMITIVE SAINTS AND THE SEE OF ROME. By F. W. PULLER, M.A., Mission Priest of the Society of St. John Evangelist, Cowley, Oxford. *Crown 8vo.* 7s. 6d.

Pusey.—LIFE OF EDWARD BOUVERIE PUSEY, D.D. By HENRY PARRY LIDDON, D.D., D.C.L., LL.D. Edited and prepared for publication by the Rev. J. O. JOHNSTON, M.A., Vicar of All Saints', Oxford, and the Rev. ROBERT J. WILSON, M.A., Warden of Keble College. *Four Vols. 8vo. Vols. I. and II., with 2 Portraits and 7 Illustrations.* 36s.

Pusey.—Works by the Rev. E. B. PUSEY, D.D.
   PRIVATE PRAYERS. With Preface by H. P. LIDDON, D.D. *32mo.* 1s.
   PRAYERS FOR A YOUNG SCHOOLBOY. With a Preface by H. P. LIDDON, D.D. *24mo.* 1s.

Sanday.—Works by W. SANDAY, D.D., Dean Ireland's Professor of Exegesis and Fellow of Exeter College, Oxford.
INSPIRATION : Eight Lectures on the Early History and Origin of the Doctrine of Biblical Inspiration. Being the Bampton Lectures for 1893. *8vo.* 16*s.*
THE ORACLES OF GOD: Nine Lectures on the Nature and Extent of Biblical Inspiration and the Special Significance of the Old Testament Scriptures at the Present Time. *Crown 8vo.* 4*s.*
TWO PRESENT-DAY QUESTIONS. I. Biblical Criticism. II. The Social Movement. Sermons preached before the University of Cambridge. *Crown 8vo.* 2*s.* 6*d.*

Seebohm.—THE OXFORD REFORMERS—JOHN COLET, ERASMUS, AND THOMAS MORE: A History of their Fellow-Work. By FREDERICK SEEBOHM. *8vo.* 14*s.*

Stanton.—THE PLACE OF AUTHORITY IN MATTERS OF RELIGIOUS BELIEF. By VINCENT HENRY STANTON, D.D., Fellow of Trinity Coll., Ely Prof. of Divinity, Cambridge. *Cr. 8vo.* 6*s.*

Swayne.—THE BLESSED DEAD IN PARADISE. Four All Saints' Day Sermons, preached in Salisbury Cathedral. By R. G. SWAYNE, M.A. *Crown 8vo.* 3*s.* 6*d.*

Twells.—COLLOQUIES ON PREACHING. By HENRY TWELLS, M.A., Honorary Canon of Peterborough. *Crown 8vo.* 2*s.* 6*d.*

Welldon.—THE FUTURE AND THE PAST. Sermons preached to Harrow Boys. By the Rev. J. E. C. WELLDON, M.A., Head Master of Harrow School. *Crown 8vo.* 7*s.* 6*d.*

Williams.—Works by the Rev. ISAAC WILLIAMS, B.D.
A DEVOTIONAL COMMENTARY ON THE GOSPEL NARRATIVE, *Eight Vols. Crown 8vo.* 5*s. each. Sold Separately.*

THOUGHTS ON THE STUDY OF THE HOLY GOSPELS.	OUR LORD'S MINISTRY (Third Year).
	THE HOLY WEEK.
A HARMONY OF THE FOUR GOSPELS.	
OUR LORD'S NATIVITY.	OUR LORD'S PASSION.
OUR LORD'S MINISTRY (Second Year).	OUR LORD'S RESURRECTION.

FEMALE CHARACTERS OF HOLY SCRIPTURE. A Series of Sermons, *Crown 8vo.* 5*s.*
THE CHARACTERS OF THE OLD TESTAMENT. *Crown 8vo.* 5*s.*
THE APOCALYPSE. With Notes and Reflections. *Crown 8vo.* 5*s.*
SERMONS ON THE EPISTLES AND GOSPELS FOR THE SUNDAYS AND HOLY DAYS. *Two Vols. Crown 8vo.* 5*s. each.*

[continued.

16   A SELECTION OF THEOLOGICAL WORKS.

Williams.—Works by the Rev. ISAAC WILLIAMS, B.D.—*continued.*
  PLAIN SERMONS ON CATECHISM. Two Vols. Cr. 8vo. 5s. each.
  SELECTIONS FROM ISAAC WILLIAMS' WRITINGS. Cr. 8vo. 3s. 6d.
  THE AUTOBIOGRAPHY OF ISAAC WILLIAMS, B.D., Author of several of the 'Tracts for the Times.' Edited by the Venerable Sir GEORGE PREVOST, as throwing further light on the history of the Oxford Movement. *Crown 8vo.* 5s.

Woodford.—Works by J. R. WOODFORD, D.D., Bishop of Ely.
  THE GREAT COMMISSION. Addresses on the Ordinal. Edited, with an Introduction, by H. M. LUCKOCK, D.D. *Crown 8vo.* 5s.
  SERMONS ON OLD AND NEW TESTAMENT SUBJECTS. Edited by H. M. LUCKOCK, D.D. Two Vols. *Crown 8vo.* 5s. each.

Wordsworth.
  For List of Works by the late Christopher Wordsworth, D.D., Bishop of Lincoln, see Messrs. Longmans & Co.'s Catalogue of Theological Works, 32 pp. Sent post free on application.

Wordsworth.—Works by ELIZABETH WORDSWORTH, Principal of Lady Margaret Hall, Oxford.
  ILLUSTRATIONS OF THE CREED. *Crown 8vo.* 5s.
  THE DECALOGUE. *Crown 8vo.* 4s. 6d.
  ST. CHRISTOPHER AND OTHER POEMS. *Crown 8vo.* 6s.

Wordsworth.—Works by CHARLES WORDSWORTH, D.D., D.C.L., Lord Bishop of St. Andrews, and Fellow of Winchester College.
  ANNALS OF MY EARLY LIFE, 1806-1846. 8vo. 15s.
  ANNALS OF MY LIFE, 1847-1856. 8vo. 10s. 6d.
  PRIMARY WITNESS TO THE TRUTH OF THE GOSPEL, to which is added a Charge on Modern Teaching on the Canon of the Old Testament. *Crown 8vo.* 7s. 6d.

Younghusband.—Works by FRANCES YOUNGHUSBAND.
  THE STORY OF OUR LORD, told in Simple Language for Children. With 25 Illustrations from Pictures by the Old Masters. *Crown 8vo.* 2s. 6d.
  THE STORY OF THE EXODUS, told in Simple Language for Children. With Map and 29 Illustrations. *Crown 8vo.* 2s. 6d.

Printed by T. and A. CONSTABLE, Printers to Her Majesty,
at the Edinburgh University Press.

www.ingramcontent.com/pod-product-compliance
Lightning Source LLC
Chambersburg PA
CBHW020108170426
43199CB00009B/445